find
fulfill
flourish

Steve Weitzenkorn
and Robin Damsky

find
fulfill
flourish

Discover Your Purpose With LifePath GPS

f3
forum

forum

Cover and interior design by Bill Greaves, Concept West.

ISBN 978-0615431765
LCCN 2010943230

FindFulfillFlourish.com

Dedication

We dedicate this work to those who have inspired us the most in life.

Steve

This is for my parents, William and Lillian Weitzenkorn, who instilled values, offered guidance for wise choices, and enabled me to pursue my dreams; my wife, Bonnie Kabin, who is my daily inspiration, best friend, encourager, and biggest fan; and my son Ben, who is charting his unique path, pursuing his passions, and living by his beliefs.

Robin

This is for my parents, Michael and Sondra Damsky, who gave me passion for life and encouraged me to pursue my dreams; my grandparents, Irma and Al Leventhal, who taught me to live a life of values and spirit; and to my daughter, Sarah, the light of my life, whose big heart is devoted to making our world a better place.

Acknowledgements

A book, like a fulfilling and productive community, is a work of collaboration, and the entire *Find Fulfill Flourish* Project is, as well. So many shared their stories with us, gave us very personal accounts of their life experiences, and generously offered their time and insight. Others offered their wisdom and skill, read and reread our pages, or gave us insight into design. Still others provided us emotional support, constantly cheering us on.

We are especially grateful to Laura Orsini, Write | Market | Design, for her guidance, insight, and innumerable suggestions for improving this work. She is much more than a great editor. We truly appreciate her expertise and ongoing commitment to making this project a success.

Others who helped make this endeavor possible or contributed to it in a meaningful way are:

Andrea Beth Damsky, Angela Thoburn, Ben Bolch, Ben Weitzenkorn, Bill Greaves, Bob Medack, Bonnie Kabin, Carol Koenig, Carolyn Manning, Craig Wolfe, David Silverman, Denise D. Resnik, Dov Peretz Elkins, Dov Vogel, Elaine Birks-Mitchell, Hannah Adelman, Helene Weitzenkorn, Hillel Levin, Jerry Toomer, Jessica Berg and the staff at the Lodestar Day Resource Center, Joryn West, Kelly and Anne Campbell, Lee Haas, Leslie Lerman, Lori Silverman, Lucie Ticho, M. Zuhdi Jasser, Martin Zamora, Michael and Sondra Damsky, Michelle Haas Seagull, Nancy Zangari, Pam Gardner, Paul Wolfman, Sarah Damsky, Scott MacKay, Stefan Pinto, Talia Browdy, Tio Hardiman, Tom Wright, and Yosef Garcia.

Think of the world you've always dreamed of.
Once we approach adulthood, we may abandon the dream,
thinking it no longer possible.

What kind of world could we create
if each one of us worked a little bit each day
toward making the world more like the one of our dreams?

If creating the world of our dreams became
an integral part our lives and our legacy to others,
imagine the lives we would touch
and how our own lives would become more meaningful.

— Robin Damsky and Steve Weitzenkorn

Contents

Chapter 1

The Personal Journey
to *Find Fulfill Flourish*

Navigating your LifePath
Living a life of meaning and fulfillment
Expressing your uniqueness

Find Fulfill Flourish is about a personal journey. It's about finding a direction and purpose, bringing that purpose to life or fulfilling it, and then both flourishing as a person, as well as helping your community to flourish. Without a guide or directional system, navigating this journey may be challenging. You're probably familiar with the concept of a GPS (Global Positioning System), a device in many cell phones, automobiles, and stand-alone tools that can tell us our precise geographical location at any given time. We use the analogy of a LifePath GPS to create a set of tools for this expedition called life.

The navigational software in the GPS guides our travel so precisely that it tells us where to turn and even recalculates our route if we go off course. This incredible technology helps us find our way. LifePath GPS is a similar system to guide us through life. This system can help set our direction and determine where we want to go. We can sometimes rely on family, friends, clergy, teachers, colleagues, coaches, bosses, professionals, or authorities for guidance. Other times, however, we may feel we are on our own. Consider how you could help yourself if you had your own internalized guidance system. What questions would you ask this system?

Many of us may feel a powerful sense of guidance from the lessons we learned growing up, our religious affiliation or spiritual path, a seminar we attended, or other influences in our lives. If this is the case for you, the information in this guide will expand that capacity and enable you to take your life to a higher level of integration, meaning, and fulfillment.

If you feel these tools have been missing or limited in your life, this book offers a guidance system you can begin using immediately, one that will remain available throughout your life. Our hope is

> At some point in our lives, we come to the realization that (a) we are living a life of meaning and purpose, or (b) we are merely being swept along by the tides around us.

that this book will serve as a thought-provoking tool to help you assess your current position on life's path and to navigate toward your desired future in a purposeful way. Use this process to help discover your purpose and begin living a life you are excited to wake up to each morning.

INTRODUCTION

At some point in our lives, we come to the realization that (a) we are living a life of meaning and purpose, or (b) we are merely being swept along by the tides around us. We wonder, "Who am I, and how do I make a difference?" Asking this question is the first step toward living with intention, and answering it brings us the true satisfaction of knowing we are living wisely and for good.

An effective and fulfilling life path is developed in stages. First, it is essential to know the general direction you wish to go and why – even though the specifics and nature of the journey may change any number of times over the course of your life. The goal, regardless of your age, is not to make hard and fast decisions about where you wish to go in life. Rather, the idea is to discover a meaningful and fulfilling life and how best to pursue it. This will enrich your life in the present, as well.

We are all unique individuals. This guide is intended to help you to become the "you" that you really want to be – to find your unique vision and fulfill the part of your life that makes flourishing possible. The objective is to help you build on and apply the unique qualities and desires that characterize who you are.

The route to a fulfilling, purpose-infused life generally is not a linear path. There are few direct routes, and even those may be filled with curves, dips, and inclines. Life usually has few straight lines.

Before you can effectively navigate your life, you must first decide "where" you want your aspirations to take you. The "where" on your LifePath GPS is not a geographical location; rather, it is a place of personal development, accomplishment, contribution, and fulfillment. You will need to develop a vision for what you wish to do with your life, recognizing that this may change and evolve as a result of accumulated life experiences and education.

The "where" most of us seek is a good life that brings us satisfaction. Meaning comes from finding a place to make a contribution and serve others. It is the feeling that what we do has value and helps the greater good. The way we find meaning is different for everyone. It may be through volunteerism, community or spiritual service, career, sports, the arts, politics, or philanthropy. We will explore all of these elements in this guide.

The GPS Metaphor and LifePath GPS Navigational Guide

GPS is a satellite-based system that uses three different coordinates to pinpoint one's position. **Longitude** is the east-west position on the earth's surface, based on one's distance from the Prime Meridian (an imaginary line connecting the North and South poles that passes though Greenwich, England). **Latitude** is the north-south position, as measured from the equator. Your **actual position** is the point where these lines intersect.

LifePath GPS also is three-dimensional, involving:

- Self-integrity
- Relationships
- Your purpose

Tracking your progress along your path is a purely subjective process, based on your own self-assessment of where you are today and your dreams of where you want to go. It is neither scientific nor mathematical; it is personal. For you to attain the most value from this process, you must be as honest as possible with yourself. Even if you feel that you have never really been on a path before, you can track your progress. You may be at the beginning of your path, or you may discover that you already are well on your journey.

This book works in tandem with a wide range of tools available on our website. At any point, you may want to access the supplemental information available at FindFulfillFlourish.com. Use Coupon Code GBC3MN24.

"The purpose of life
is a life of purpose."
— Robert Byrne

How to Use the LifePath GPS Guide

We have designed this book and the accompanying tools to help you give voice to the questions you may have about creating meaning in your life. These questions will help you generate ideas about your **Beliefs**, **Intentions**, **Behavior**, and **Impact** (BIBI) that will lead to a more personally meaningful life, one that resonates with your individuality.

Most of the chapters in this book have three sections:

- **A true story about a person whose actions exemplify the concepts central to the chapter.** Some of the stories are about people with strong religious/spiritual beliefs or political leanings, both on the left and the right. Whether you agree or disagree with them philosophically is of little importance. We encourage you to focus less on their faith or the causes they champion, and to concentrate instead on the characteristics that illustrate the key concepts.

- **The *Find*, *Fulfill*, or *Flourish* premise of the chapter.** Embracing these principles and integrating them into your path will help you lead a more meaningful and purposeful life.

- **Questions and practical tools for helping you explore the concepts as they apply to your life, and ways to implement them.** Certain chapters refer you to the website for expanded exercises and tools. We strongly urge you to do the exercises at the end of each chapter as you read them, rather than putting them aside to "come back to later."

LIFEPATH GPS MODEL and EIGHT DYNAMICS

LifePath GPS, like the GPS in cars and cell phones, is based on a system of interrelated parts. LifePath incorporates Eight Dynamics, as illustrated below.

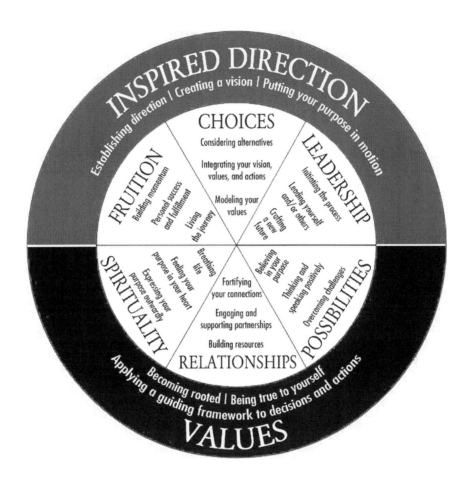

Together, these Dynamics define who we are and how satisfied we are with our lives. They do not operate in isolation from each other, but in symbiotic combination as a life system. Each dynamic impacts the others; they are synergistic. One chapter is devoted to each dynamic. As you consider these Dynamics, think about how each affects the others, and your life overall.

Values: The values you practice daily define who you are and form the foundation for your LifePath. Values are foundational, and therefore are shown supporting and embracing the other Dynamics. [Chapter 4]

Inspired Direction: Establishing your direction sets the course for your journey, and your actions propel you along the path. This dynamic is aspirational, and is shown at the top of the model because it focuses on moving you forward purposefully. [Chapter 5]

Spirituality: It's about breathing and connecting to a purpose that is greater than you, and emanating outwardly the commitment you feel deep inside. [Chapter 6]

Relationships: Our relationships are precious, and most of the great things in life are achieved with and through other people. Our LifePath and the LifePaths of others are inextricably interwoven. [Chapter 7]

Living Possibilities: Believing in possibilities and what can be achieved is essential to accomplishing challenging goals. Positive thinking and communication are key ingredients for jumping the hurdles we may encounter. [Chapter 8]

Life Leadership: First, we must lead our own lives. Only then can we lead others. Leadership is about taking initiative and choosing to shape the future, rather than allowing the past, current circumstances, or others to define it. [Chapter 9]

Choices: In essence, you are the sum of your choices, and your choices reflect your true values. Both our life-altering choices and the moment-to-moment decisions we make significantly determine the course of our LifePath. [Chapter 10]

Passion to Action to Fruition: This capstone dynamic is about the process of moving from passion to action to fruition. Inspirational energy needs to be constructively channeled to create value and make a difference. Converting your inspiration into meaningful actions is essential to living a meaningful, fulfilling, and flourishing life. [Chapter 11]

The worksheet on the opposite page will give you a better idea of how you prioritize the Eight Dynamics.

LifePath GPS Self-Assessment

Take a few minutes to complete the following self-assessment. Where you place yourself on each of the three LifePath GPS dimensions and their associated sub-dimensions will give you a good sense of where you are on your life's journey.

MY SELF-INTEGRITY	VERY WEAK	WEAK	SO-SO	STRONG	VERY STRONG	GOAL(S) AND ACTION STEPS
True to My Values						
Spirituality						
My Choices						

MY RELATIONSHIPS	VERY UNFULFILLING	UNFULFILLING	SO-SO	FULFILLING	VERY FULFILLING	GOAL(S) AND ACTION STEPS
Family						
Friends & Acquaintances						
Coworkers						
Incidental People/Encounters						
Strangers						

MY PURPOSE	VERY WEAK	WEAK	SO-SO	STRONG	VERY STRONG	GOAL(S) AND ACTION STEPS
Engaging Others						
Personal Commitment						
Efforts to Date						
Living Possibilities						
Life Leadership						
Personal Fulfillment						

A printer-friendly version of this worksheet is available on our website. Visit FindFulfillFlourish.com, find the Book & Tools tab, and click on Additional Application Exercises.

To gauge how accurate your self-assessment is, you may wish to discuss it with close friends and people you trust to give you honest, objective feedback; these individuals will not "tell you what to do," but rather help you discern your path. The following steps may be helpful:

INNER QUEST
What would make your life meaningful?

OUTER QUEST
What have you done — or could you do — that would be meaningful and fulfilling?

- Seek others' opinions and input.
- Listen carefully and check that you understand precisely what they mean to convey.
- Be open and receptive to what they say.
- Ask them for examples to illustrate their points.
- Consider how well their perceptions align with your own.
- Make adjustments based on their input.

View this as a reality check and an opportunity to be truly honest with yourself. Remember, however, that as helpful as others' input may be, your life decisions are yours to determine and act on. Consider their feedback, but know that you are the master and decisionmaker for your life.

Completing this self-assessment will mark the departure point for the next leg of your journey. Though the task of charting your position, both today and in the future, may seem formidable, when you break it down into smaller pieces, it becomes less intimidating – and far more exciting and attainable.

Making the Most of Your *Find Fulfill Flourish* Experience

This book is not theoretical. If you truly desire to make a change in your life – to find your life's purpose and live a life of passion and meaning – all the tools are at your fingertips, either right here in the book, or on FindFulfillFlourish.com. We suggest you grab your favorite notebook (or purchase a journal at FindFulfillFlourish.com/Store) and do the exercises at the end of each chapter, titled APPLYING THE CONCEPTS TO YOUR LIFE. Visit the website for further exercises and tools. If you read the book without taking the time to do the exercises, this information will remain theoretical, or simply a nice idea. But if you take the time to go through this process and do the work, you will identify your LifePath and be well on your way to living a fulfilled life of purpose.

NAVIGATIONAL POINTS

- Keys to a meaningful life include finding your purpose, taking action to fulfill it, and helping others flourish so that you can, as well.

- Creating a direction is an essential part of the process; however, keep in mind that your direction may change, and you are very likely to make mid-course adjustments.

- LifePath GPS is a metaphor to help us understand where we are and where we want to go.

- The three LifePath GPS dimensions are self-integrity, relationships, and personal purpose.

- The Eight Dynamics comprise a system for navigating our journey.

APPLYING THE CONCEPTS TO YOUR LIFE

1. What are your personal objectives for reading this book?
2. How would you like to flourish?

"When you are inspired by some great purpose,
some extraordinry project,
all your thoughts break their bonds;
your mind transcends limitations,
your consciousness expands in every direction,
and you find yourself in a new, great, and wonderful world.
Dormant forces, faculties, and talents become alive,
and you discover yourself to be a greater person by far
than you ever dreamed yourself to be."
— Patanjali

Chapter 2

The Journey to Find Meaning and Become a "Heartisan"

Defining who you are

Discovering what it means to be a "heartisan"

Integrating heartisanship into your personal DNA

Sarah's Identity and Commitment: Beginning a Life Journey

A ten-year-old girl tells Sarah how scary it was to know that her dad was being hunted by the Mexican Mafia. Another young girl shares that her mother, a single teenager when the girl was born, is struggling to both work and attend school while taking care of her. A daughter of illegal immigrants describes how her parents were victims of police brutality and that she hasn't seen them in years. Another discloses that her mother is an alcoholic and how tense this makes life at home.

Sarah is a high school student who volunteers at Camp Swift, which offers free overnight camping experiences to economically disadvantaged children. Children are bused from Phoenix to the camp in the Prescott National Forest in Arizona, where they spend four to five days in the fresh mountain air. For the first time in their lives, these fourth, fifth, and sixth graders are away from the concrete jungle of the city, and find themselves deposited into the midst of gigantic Ponderosa pines.

Many campers arrive with false bravado, acting tough. Sarah is moved that these elementary school girls, who have known her for only a day or two, trust her enough to disclose such intimate details about their lives. These heart-wrenching stories touch Sarah deeply. She refers to them as a "flash of moments" that remind her how much help these children need. Hearing their stories conjures a mix of emotions. Sarah knows there is little more she can do than listen and be a friend, yet she feels deep compassion for these girls. The camp session ends, and Sarah experiences a sense of accomplishment and loss.

While Sarah knows she has had an impact, she feels a "momentary relief but not pardon" – there is still so much to do, and she feels even further compelled to help. This is the paradox of fulfillment for Sarah and many others on their LifePath: she is pleased to have helped, but is increasingly aware of the great needs that remain.

Sarah explains, "Just because you are helping children doesn't mean you are solving the problem." It's like treating the symptoms of a virus, rather than curing it. "Suppressing the symptoms won't get rid of the problem."

This realization motivates Sarah to a higher level of service. Her sense of fulfillment and accomplishment inspire her to do more. And the cycle keeps perpetuating itself. As Sarah says, "I briefly acknowledge myself, pick up, and continue." She also notes that she has not done this work by herself – others are involved. "I did not start my work helping others alone – I was never alone." Knowing that others on the team are also deeply engaged makes the entire undertaking that much more powerful and significant.

Sarah believes in the catalyst effect – creating a "pay it forward" chain reaction, referencing the belief in repaying a good deed you receive by helping someone, even a stranger, and encouraging that person to help someone else, thereby radiating waves of kindness. The more people who embrace this value as a personal commitment, the greater the good and the greater the impact.

Sarah's deep commitment and awareness of issues are striking for a seventeen-year-old. Although her journey has been underway for a few years and she has direction, Sarah is also just getting started. She is very involved in community service and social action initiatives, and the more she does, the more inspired and committed she becomes. She has already been involved in numerous social service projects and is especially drawn to helping children living with very difficult circumstances.

In recognizing that her actions are fueling her passion, Sarah wants to devote her life to making a difference. To equip herself for this adventure, she is planning a college major in nonprofit management. However, she has already launched herself on a purpose-infused path, and you can feel the power of her motivation.

Sarah conveys a sense of pride and self-confidence in the person she is. In part, these reflect her youthful exuberance and inclination to explore new ideas, remain open minded, learn from experience, and spread her wings. She is developing her own voice and seems to recognize that this is a work in progress. Accompanying this new phase is another evolving aspect of Sarah's character, which she describes as "thinking about things more rationally than in the past." Perhaps her strengthened rationality, coupled with her "let's try everything" disposition, is the source of her healthy confusion.

Sarah realizes she is still figuring things out and that her direction may change as she grows and matures. However, she has a very good idea of who she is, what she wants to be, and the general direction she wants to go. She is simultaneously grounded and animated. Her core values are proactivity, compassion, and rationality. She describes rationality as "not just thinking about yourself, but really thinking things through and then doing something." Sarah is combining purpose with action to make a difference. She believes it is important for everyone to find something that inspires them, even if it makes them uncomfortable at first. As she says, "Just do something."

This outlook is integral to Sarah's life philosophy. She reflects on times she has felt uncomfortable and perhaps had a sense of insecurity, saying, "I remind myself that everyone is equal and human. People don't always expect you to do something, sometimes they just want you to listen."

For Sarah, listening is important; she expresses her love in the doing.

For more information about Camp Swift, visit campswift.org.

The Journey Begins With Who You Are

From Lewis Carroll's classic *Alice's Adventures in Wonderland*:

> **Alice:** *Who in the world am I? Ah, THAT'S the great puzzle!*
>
> *She generally gave herself very good advice, though she very seldom followed it.*
>
> **Caterpillar:** *Who are you?*

Alice: I – I hardly know, Sir, just at present – at least I know who I was ... but I think I must have been changed several times since then.

Caterpillar: What do you mean by that? Explain yourself!

Alice: I can't explain myself, I'm afraid, Sir, because I'm not myself, you see.

Caterpillar: I don't see.

Alice: I'm afraid I can't put it more clearly, for I can't understand it myself.

How many of us are like Alice, wondering who we are, where we are, why we are here, how we got here, and whether or not we are lost? Is it possible that the way you have been defining yourself no longer suits you? But perhaps you are unsure about how to redefine yourself and who you would like to become. How often do we diminish ourselves by pretending to be someone we are not? How many of us cannot explain ourselves, wonder about our purpose in life, or question the meaning of our life? We wonder if this is all there is. Many of us want to know how we can get more out of life, how to make our lives much more meaningful than they already are.

> If someone asked you, "Where are you on life's journey?" could you answer without saying something about your age, education, career, or wealth?

This book explores ways to respond to these questions. It's important to realize that each of us has our own unique answers. Our individual Beliefs, Intentions, Behavior, and Impact (BIBI) – are at the center of who we are. One of the concluding chapters, "Passion to Action to Fruition," crystallizes the connection between the Eight Dynamics and our identity.

If someone asked you, "Where are you on life's journey?" could you answer without saying something about your age, education, career, or wealth? People commonly respond to this query with a puzzled look, followed by a question such as, "What else is there?" when you press them for something beyond these obvious responses.

Answers to the "what else" question address the most meaningful aspects of life. They define not only where we are but who we are, and then create the motivation that gets us out of bed in the morning on those days when we don't have to work, that feeling that happens when you do something for someone without asking anything in return, or when you've done the right thing in a difficult situation. It is the spirit that defines why you are here, and what you will leave behind when you are gone – something that is you, but also much bigger than you.

Think about parents of babies and young children. They often seem to have a glow about them. Having welcomed a new life into their family, they depict a sense of fulfillment and joy, perhaps greater than they have known in some time. Through their children, they have taken on a commitment greater than themselves; it is about more than love. They have created a new purpose for their lives – that of caring for and raising their children, helping them to become successful people in their own right. Each step toward this goal, whether small or large, give parents deep fulfillment and happiness. In raising children, parents often find meaning and purpose.

Parenthood and its attendant responsibilities become a springboard for pursuing meaningful endeavors – and simultaneously represent something much greater than oneself, because effective parenting requires us to think beyond ourselves all the time. As parents, we *must* put our focus on our children. With the onset of family, we instantly find ourselves in the position of having created something bigger than ourselves. Raising a family gives some people their first true sense of purpose and working to improve something outside of themselves. In fact, many people who discover a purposeful existence through family go on to devote themselves to other kinds of service.

One fascinating aspect of our collaboration is that Robin, as a rabbi, lives her life from a faith-based orientation: God plays a prominent role in her experiences and life path. Steve, while based in a religious tradition, utilizes a secular approach to finding meaning in his life.

You will hear both authors' voices throughout this guide. This is done intentionally in an effort to be inclusive of all perspectives as you embark on charting your LifePath journey. We hope that at least one – if not both – perspectives will help guide you.

Regardless of whether your perspective more closely aligns with that of Robin or Steve, our central premise is that we develop meaning in our lives through intention and action. You may or may not be motivated by a higher power or spirituality. Nevertheless, you can gain fulfillment through the deep reward you receive from caring for and investing in something outside of yourself.

This is but one way of discovering a path to deeper meaning; there are many, many others. In fact, there are as many ways to design a rich life as there are people in the world. Some learn about the value of service when they are young, as they watch their families help the sick or clothe the poor. For others, the joy of reaching out may come from spending an afternoon with a friend who volunteers at a homeless shelter. For others still, service is learned in a church, synagogue, or mosque. It may come from wanting to see a cure for a chronic illness or from seeing injustice and knowing in your bones that it is wrong. It may come from a love of the earth and its beauty.

Your personal springboard to creating a deeply fulfilling, meaningful life could come from exposure to ideas, life experiences, serendipitous opportunities, and even a personal or family trauma. For example, Linda Bergendahl-Pauling created the Make-A-Wish Foundation, along with Frank Shankwitz and Scott Stahl, after her seven-year-old son, Chris, died of leukemia.

Examples that are profiled in subsequent chapters of this book include:

Denise D. Resnik established the Southwest Autism Research & Resource Center (SARRC), with Dr. Cindy Schneider and Dr. Raun Melmed, to help children and families with autism.

Belief in a higher power, alone, is not enough. Robin's grandmother always used repeat the famous line, "God helps those who help themselves." This means that God requires your partnership and investment in making this world a better place. This is a major tenet of the Jewish tradition, in which God created people to be partners in building and perfecting this world. Big job!

A more secular approach is seen in Steve's view. He believes that while God may have a role in determining our purpose, we can also develop a meaningful lives without such belief. Steve says that the real work is up to us, that the inspiration may come from within us or be triggered by events in our lives. He believes the important question is not, "What is the meaning of life?" but rather "What meaning can we put into life?"

Kelly and Anne Campbell founded The Village Experience, an organization that offers travelers an inside experience of villages and their inhabitants in underdeveloped countries and created a fair trade store for selling crafts.

Elaine Birks-Mitchell, after discovering the need, began The Bra Recyclers, a business that collects and donates thousands of bras to women's shelters in Arizona, around the country, and around the world.

Yosef Garcia was raised a Catholic in Panama before discovering his Jewish heritage, converting to Judaism, and becoming a rabbi. He now helps other "Crypto Jews" who wish to return to the religion of their ancestors.

Each of these individuals discovered a need and turned it into a project that was useful not only to themselves, but to others as well. Each of them began by seeing an opportunity to make a positive difference. Some evolved from unfortunate personal circumstances, others from seeing a need in the community. Your passion can come from a positive transformational experience, a personal challenge, your faith, or the simple desire to make the world a better place. While these stories profile people who launched large undertakings, we also will be providing examples of individuals who pursued a meaningful purpose in more modest ways, through volunteering and other endeavors that suited their busy schedules and lifestyles.

Many find their inspiration for meaning and purpose through their belief in God or a higher power. Rick Warren, in his best-seller, *Purpose Driven Life*, sees this as integral to the process. He quotes Bertrand Russell, an atheist, to reinforce his point: "Unless you assume a God, the question of life's purpose is meaningless." Though a belief in God is central to many people's discovery of their life purpose, many other paths do exist. This guide will help you find your path, whether or not spirituality or religion plays a role in your life.

Thomas Jefferson, author of the United States' Declaration of Independence, wrote the famous phrase that all people are "endowed … with certain unalienable rights, that among these are life, liberty, and the pursuit of happiness." The wording Jefferson uses is significant. We are given life by our parents, and enlightened government can grant us liberty; however we, as individuals, must take it upon ourselves to pursue happiness. We have the choice to seek happiness; if we value it, pursuing it becomes a personal responsibility. It is also a continual process. The same can be said for the pursuit of self-fulfillment. The opportunities and choices continually appear for us to explore.

Ultimately, we must take responsibility for finding and achieving a fulfilling life, as elusive as that process may be. Self-fulfillment cannot be granted to us; we must develop it on our own by living a purposeful life that reflects our values. This pursuit of self-fulfillment and meaning is not a destination, but rather a journey that continues throughout life.

Becoming a "Heartisan"

The word "artisan" calls to mind a person who works in the arts, a trade, or a craft. Artisans usually have a commitment to their work and a true love for it. They create new aesthetic works out of raw materials. They often take ordinary objects and raise them to a greater level of beauty or give them a new meaning or purpose. Artisans express themselves through their creative energy and devotion.

INNER QUEST
What's in your heart?

OUTER QUEST
How can you follow your heart to make a difference?

A "heartisan" has very similar characteristics. Heartisans have a sincere commitment to a worthy cause, which may involve improving the lives of others, their community, or the general well-being. They have a heartfelt devotion to a purpose greater than themselves and the courage, energy, and spirit to pursue it. Heartisans work for the betterment of others and/or the world as an expression of their "heart." This devotion and work become intricately woven into their LifePath.

The stories in this book illustrate the commitment of individuals who have become heartisans. Denise Resnik's heart moved her to find answers for her autistic son and for others like him. Kelly Campbell's heart guided her to help eliminate poverty by facilitating independence and dignity for people who would otherwise be dependent. Elaine Birks-Mitchell's heart is so big that she devotes an enormous amount of personal time to support women who have been crushed by abuse. Rabbi Garcia wants to help those whose religious paths were deterred by tyranny to open their hearts to the religion of their ancestors.

Heartisans' hearts guide them to make meaningful contributions. Finding your path and determining the unique contribution you want to make will bring forth the heartisan within you.

In every story you will find an individual who has listened to his or her heart and created a life of meaning. In every case, the individual found meaning and fulfillment through their heart's desire to help others or make a difference in their own unique way. We believe that any person who embodies the essential characteristics of a heartisan is on a LifePath of significance, whether in their job, the arts, philanthropy, volunteering, sports, political action, or another way. Choosing work that moves your heart and makes a positive difference for others will continue to refuel you, day after day, and have a positive effect on the world.

Reflection

Do you know where you are in your life? Do you know where you are in your pursuit of self-fulfillment? Do you have a purpose that inspires you, one that may challenge you to the depths of your heart and gives you satisfaction when you achieve even a small gain? Do you feel called from your heart to make a positive and meaningful difference? If so, what is it? If not, do you feel like Alice – a lost soul?

This book is intended to help you answer these questions for yourself; questions people have been asking themselves for centuries:

- Who am I?
- Who do I aspire to be?
- What is my purpose?
- Where do I wish to go with my life?
- How do I make my life more meaningful?

The answers to these questions help us anchor ourselves and form a key segment of our identity – a sense of self and confidence in who we are. In Chapter 12, "Forward Navigation: Who Am I Becoming?" we offer specific guidance on answering the "Who am I?" question.

When all is said and done, how will you know that you are satisfied with the life you lived? If you identify with Alice, you may see yourself as a "lost soul." This term is often used to describe people who feel adrift, people who do not know where they are in life, what they want from it, or what is meaningful to them. Does this sound like you? Is it possible to be a lost soul and not realize it? Most importantly, if you are a lost soul, how can you rediscover yourself?

In today's fast-paced world, the pressures of school, job/career, raising a family, making ends meet, and life's myriad other issues make it very easy to feel adrift and lose sight of what is really important. You may feel you are simply going through the motions of life or living out unconscious choices. if that is the case, ask yourself:

- What would a meaningful life look like to me?
- Am I being true to myself and authentic?
- Am I the person I really want to be?
- Is my heart involved in the matter?

Exploring the answers to these questions can help you attain the fulfillment you seek.

Quite possibly, your life is so busy that you have never thought to ask yourself these questions, or you feel you have no time to address such weighty topics. Furthermore, the stresses of day-to-day living may interfere with the very things you value most.

Defining who you are, determining your purpose, and propelling yourself in a meaningful way is a journey in itself. It is an ever-evolving process that will likely deepen and broaden as you mature as an individual. During this personal discovery progression, your identity and self-perception will likely evolve and change as you accumulate life experiences, insights, accomplishments, and wisdom. Finally, it may be the one thing that allows the "busy-ness" of your life come into a natural sense of order.

In our view, WHO you are, as opposed to WHAT you are, is a combination or the four factors we mentioned earlier: your beliefs, intentions, behavior, and impact (BIBI). Determining the purpose you wish to pursue usually springs from your beliefs, including personal values, and intentions. They represent, in essence, your "heart." Living them is achieved though your behavior and the impact of accumulated actions.

Susanna Marcos, a principal in a successful business consulting firm in Spain, raised a very pertinent question: "Do we need a purpose?"

No, we do not technically need a purpose. One can get through life easily without finding fulfillment or meaning on any significant level. It is our premise, however, that a purpose is fundamental for living a meaningful, fulfilling life. Purpose moves us beyond the ordinary, toward the extraordinary – in our life experiences, the value we create, and the gratification we receive from living.

> "It takes courage to grow up and be who you really are."
> —— e.e. cummings

Finding and pursuing a purpose intersects

with self-interest; the two are inextricably intertwined. Performing good works, striving to achieve meaningful goals, or being a role model in one's career or in government, politics, business, the arts, and other fields can also be advantageous personally. Committing to a purpose beyond yourself generates tangible and intangible benefits, such as relationships, personal satisfaction, recognition, emulation, and a legacy. The rewards may not be immediate or financial. We define self-interest more broadly, and over a longer time horizon. We believe these rewards are the most profound. A key to producing them is matching your efforts to your personal interests and passions.

Many people spend a good portion of their lives becoming educated so they can land good-paying jobs. They work at those jobs for decades, perhaps never even wondering whether they are happy or fulfilled. For such people, by the time they are ready to enjoy the fruits of their labor, it's almost too late. Life is not something to be endured for the reward of retirement; it should be thoroughly enjoyed, embraced, and infused with meaning and value – from start to finish. Work can and should be meaningful and personally rewarding, especially when most of us spend such a large percentage of our waking hours in the workplace.

Sometimes we need to create breathing room and space to determine what we really want for our lives; after doing so, we must take time and thought to create it. We may need to make different choices to create that space. Rather than spending countless hours on the job, perhaps it's time to step back, shift your focus, and put your life and values in perspective.

For example, you may require a complete change of environment, the opportunity to watch the city disappear in your rearview mirror as you get away for a few days. Exchange four walls for a thousand trees or a zillion grains of sand. While you are away, connect with your heart. Listen to its voice, noticing where and how it calls you to act. Or instead, donate a day to the less fortunate, perhaps working at a food bank or volunteering as a tutor for disadvantaged children. Get involved in the community where your passion lies, whether it's in sports or the arts or politics. Whichever way you do it, the idea is to step away from the daily activities that absorb you so that you can reflect and gain a new perspective. Our search for meaning intersects with our passions and values.

Many unmet needs and worthy causes exist in the world, and new ones continue to emerge locally, regionally, nationally, and globally. Robin's teacher, Angela Thoburn, used to say, "Anything worth committing your life to will not be fully achieved in your lifetime." Such a thought may seem discouraging at first, but it shouldn't be. Many great historical figures furthered their important work only so far, laying the foundation to be carried on by others who followed them. It is significant to note that this is part of what defines their great legacies.

A contemporary example of this is the emergence of the benefit rock concert. This is an idea that really took off in 1971 when George Harrison conceived and produced the Concert for Bangladesh at Madison Square Garden in New York City. It raised nearly $245,000 and set in motion the idea that musicians and artists can use their talents to support worthy causes and promote a greater good. Harrison's legacy can be seen in all the benefit concerts, organized subsequently by other famous artists, that have raised millions of dollars over the years.

INNER QUEST

How would you describe your character, greater purpose, values, and vision to illustrate the essence of WHO you are?

OUTER QUEST

How do you project that essence to others?

Some of the most notable examples include: the Music for UNICEF Concert initiated by Robert Stigwood, the Bee Gees, and Robert Frost; the Nuclear Disarmament Rally in New York City, featuring Jackson Brown, Linda Ronstadt, and Bruce Springsteen; Live Aid, organized by Bob Geldof; Farm Aid, organized Willie Nelson and John Mellencamp; and the 2010 Hope for Haiti, led by Wyclef Jean to aid victims of the massive earthquake. These professional performers were artists who made a commitment to help others, especially those with very limited ability to help themselves. Their careers were not focused on aiding the disadvantaged or saving lives, yet that is what they accomplished. George Harrison created the momentum and it continues to this day, years after his death.

Perhaps, like George Harrison and many others, we will be able to create something lasting in our lifetimes that will inspire others well into the future to follow our example and continue the journey. You need not be rich and famous, simply committed and passionate. That's the key to creating a truly enduring legacy.

First, however, we must find our purpose and begin our journey.

How do we discover that purpose? Think about those ideas, visions, or activities for which you have passion. It could be as global as ending world hunger or as local as bringing a smile to a child in the hospital. Your journey begins with your first step, whether your goal is to pick up the cause of those who have gone before you or to create a new path altogether.

Kathryn is an attorney who works for a municipal government. Her passion is bird watching, or "birding," as she calls it. She has raised thousands of dollars for conservation organizations and led hundreds of walks for church groups, hiking clubs, senior centers, libraries, and many others. Kathryn teaches at Arizona State University and in the noncredit program at Mesa Community College in Mesa, Arizona. She also helps establish and maintain "Important Bird Areas," donates walks for charity auctions, and teaches at Arizona nature festivals. Additionally, Kathryn enjoys helping people with their birding questions via e-mail and traveling to beautiful and remote spots. Her favorite feedback includes the comments: "This has been so healing for me," and "Because of you, I've decided to become a volunteer." Kathryn demonstrates how, even in our free time, our passion can become our purpose.

What are your interests? What makes you come alive? How can you turn a mere interest into a deeper passion, using your skills, abilities, and knowledge? Before undertaking a search for meaning on an organizational, community, or societal level, start by taking a self-inventory and exploring what makes you come alive.

Here are some questions to consider:

- If you ascribe to a faith, what does it teach about creating a meaningful life?
- Which values are most important to you?
- Which needs, causes, or activities do you relate to?
- Where are your empathies?
- What stirs your heart, bringing out your inner "heartisan?"
- What do your parents, family, and friends find meaningful?
- What impact do you wish to have on others?

Let your thoughts about these questions steep for a while and percolate in your mind and heart. Your purpose could be almost anything; it can be whatever you want it to be. It will likely have an effect on those you care about, as well as those who care about you. It may impact those whose paths you cross along your journey, or with whom you travel for only a short time. It may touch those you do not know. It may affect those who will come after you, as well as those you will ultimately leave behind. How will you make your life valuable to them ... a blessing, gift, or source of inspiration for them? The answer will determine your legacy.

M. Scott Peck, in his book *In Search of Stones*, explains that most things in life are multiply determined. That is, several factors or events contribute to their creation. Most likely, a number of things have contributed to making you who you are today. They may have occurred sequentially, concurrently, or both. Additionally, your reactions to events or issues play a key role in determining your purpose and your future. Wherever you are, the journey on which you are about to embark – or have already begun – is about locating and developing that aspect of yourself that is ultimately demonstrated though your actions.

It may seem at this stage of the book that we are posing more questions than providing answers. As you make your way through this process, you will encounter even more questions – but more importantly, as you continue this work, you will begin to find and form your own answers. They will reflect your individuality, values, and life experiences. The stories, ideas, suggestions, and exercises in this book will guide you, but your self-reflection and thought will ultimately reveal your unique life purpose.

It's Like DNA

The journey toward creating meaning is like the helix of the double-stranded DNA molecule. The two strands twist around themselves through thousands of molecular links that bridge the space between them. The search for meaning and purpose is similar, connecting the links of identity, personal history and experience, values, interests, heart, likes and dislikes, education, spirituality, personal relationships, the environment, and the many other intangibles that compose our lives and world.

The helix can also be a powerful visual metaphor of your meaningful life. Picture the helix strands becoming

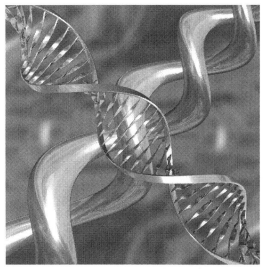

Compare the widening helix to the way your purpose blossoms as your impact grows and touches more lives.

thicker and stronger as your passion and purpose solidify. Similarly, the helix may widen as your impact becomes greater and touches more lives.

But I Already Have a Purpose

This discussion of finding and fulfilling your life's purpose is not limited to those who may feel lost or are searching to fill a void. You may already be living a purpose-inspired life. We celebrate you for your progress, and remind you that the ideas, concepts, and guidance offered in this book will strengthen your ability to pursue your personal mission. The process contained in these pages may further inspire and strengthen the momentum that fuels your pursuit.

As long as we believe in possibilities, breakthroughs will occur that profoundly affect our own life, the lives of others, and the world at large. Believing in possibilities, finding fulfillment, living with heart, and flourishing go hand-in-hand.

NAVIGATIONAL POINTS

- You can begin your journey from wherever you are.
- Inspiration can come from any place or many places.
- Fulfillment evolves from the meaning you put into life.
- Become a "heartisan."
- Envision a positive future.
- You can initiate an endeavor, continue something begun by others, or work with within an existing organization.
- Take the first step by identifying a purpose that is meaningful for you.

QUESTIONS TO CONSIDER AS YOU BEGIN OR CONTINUE YOUR JOURNEY

1. What inspires you?
2. What is meaningful for you?
3. How would you describe where you are now?
4. What are your personal objectives for reading this book?
5. How would you like to flourish?
6. If you feel you are already on your path, what is your direction?
7. How would you like to begin or continue your journey?

Chapter 3

Where to Begin

Beginning now from where you are now
Finding what inspires and invigorates you
Inspiring others as you pursue your purpose

Starting With the Joy of Giving: Dov Vogel

A woman being treated for cancer looked well, despite the fact that she had no hair. More notably, she always wore a big smile. One day, Dov Vogel walked into her treatment room. He had barely said hello when she turned and asked her husband to hand her a large medical file. She opened the file to the first page, where she had written in colorful letters a quote from Monty Python: "Always look on the bright side of life." She held the file out to Dov, showing him the four pictures she had affixed to the page: one of herself and her husband, one of herself and her children, one of herself and her grandchildren, and finally, one of herself with Dov. Amid those very personal family pictures, she had included a photo of herself with this man, barely more than a stranger. Why? Because he had made her cancer journey more bearable simply by following his life's purpose. Dov Vogel volunteers as a medical clown.

Dov says, "I am convinced that I began my life as a clown when I was born." He said this although he originally practiced a different profession, one that involved teaching and caring for others. However, in 2004, while Dov was between jobs, his daughter saw an ad in the newspaper for a course on becoming a medical clown. She told her father it would be perfect for him. Dov decided to go through with the interview so he could learn more. When he arrived at the first class, he was pleasantly surprised to find that he knew the person registering the applicants. He took that as a positive sign.

Dov was accepted into the course and soon found himself studying with young men and women many years his junior. He wasn't intimidated, however, because while he lacked their youth, he had more than thirty years of experience working with people.

When Dov finished the course, he interned at the Schneider Medical Center for Children in Israel. "The course requirement stated that I had to volunteer once a week, but I enjoyed it so much that I went twice a week. I did not have anyone supervising me, so I learned what worked by trial and error. Smiles on the part of patients, family, and hospital staff were indications that I was succeeding." And so it was that Dov built his clowning repertoire, providing solace for people in many difficult situations.

Dov's professional life picked up again, taking him away from clowning, but the joy of it stayed with him, as well as the hope that he would one day return. Several years later, he saw an opportunity at Meir Medical Center in central Israel. He asked the staff there if he could volunteer as a medical clown, and received a hearty "Yes!" Dov began clowning once a week, getting to know the staff and the patients.

"The nurse who oversaw my integration into the hospital seemed to be afraid of putting me in 'difficult' places," Dov explains. "So I started out in a few quiet areas of outpatient clinics. I asked to go to cardiology, but her response was, 'No, that is too difficult.' Perhaps because she had overseen paid clowns working in the children's ward, she did not understand the need for all people in the hospital to smile or laugh."

Dov decided to visit the cardiology department on his own. He introduced himself to the secretary and told her that he wanted to volunteer on a weekly basis. She asked him to return the following week, as she would have to speak to the physician in charge. Upon Dov's return, he was immediately visiting patients, and clowning with the doctors, nurses, and patients' families.

Dov had found his avocation. As he moved from department to department, he was invariably stopped in the corridor by nurses, who would ask, "Why don't you come to my department?" His simple answer was, "I have not yet been invited," to which the common response was, "Consider yourself invited!"

Following this simple ritual, Dov eventually incorporated obstetrics, eye care, the recovery room, and the ICU into his weekly visits. When his time allowed, he visited the rest of the wards, as well. Since the children's ward hires paid clowns, Dov didn't take his tricks there. He did, however, have the opportunity to clown around with children in the outpatient clinic and emergency room.

> "I have the opportunity to impact people's lives. I bring smiles to the faces of the patients and help them to forget and minimize their pain or fears."

Dov says, "Each week, I have the opportunity to impact people's lives. I bring smiles to the faces of the patients and help them to forget and minimize their pain or fears. I see some patients almost every week, like those in outpatient oncology and dialysis. There they sit, hooked up to drips or to a machine," some of them literally fighting for their lives. "I bring smiles to their faces, ask them how they are, and offer them a wish for their speedy recovery." What a difference Dov makes for these individuals.

"Her cancer beat her shortly after that encounter, and she died," Dov says of Mary, the woman whose story opened this chapter. "But my breath was taken away. I had seen her perhaps six times, and yet I had made a strong enough impact on her that she chose to include our picture together in her medical file.

"And I am sure that whoever looked at her medical file, whether it was a doctor, nurse, or a family member, understood that sometimes strangers have the ability to strengthen a person's hope. We may not always achieve victory, but each day of trying to live a full life is a small victory."

Dov explains his understanding of the process of finding fulfillment. "The reward of a good deed is a good deed. I leave after a shift exhausted, but I leave with a sense that I have, for a short period, made the world a better place. I have eased the tension of the nurses in the intensive care unit and at times I have gotten patients on respirators to respond, either through hand motions or eye movement. Has this led to their recovery? I don't know and I don't ask. I just have to be there. Psychology teaches that a patient who believes that he can be cured has a better chance of living longer. If a patient sees that a stranger cares about him, it will hopefully give him additional encouragement for a speedy recovery.

"Not everyone feels comfortable in a hospital. I understand this. It is not easy. Life is fragile, and anyone can find himself in a life threatening situation or simply a situation that can lead to a great deal of worry and consternation. I can think of no greater challenge in life than to help to ease the pain of one's fellow man."

Dov is a heartisan. He clowns around with people in the hospital because he simply "has to" in order to fill his own soul. Dov believed he was born to be a clown, yet the fire of his inspiration was lit by his daughter. It was his beginning, and through it he discovered his purpose. Taking action took Dov the rest of the way, as his behavior led to a profound impact on the patients and hospital staff he encountered. Every day, his hospital clowning creates joy in patients' lives, regardless of how sick or how old they are. With each visit, Dov touches the patients and their families. With each visit his fulfillment grows, as the patients and their families touch his life as well.

For further information about medical clown programs, please visit www.humourfoundation.com.au, www.slappysplayhouse.com/foundation.html, and http://bit.ly/iidp68.

The Cycle of Inspiration and Personal Fulfillment

So where do you begin? The good news is that you can begin right now, from one of many starting points. All you need is the initiative to begin.

Each point on the "Cycle of Inspiration and Personal Fulfillment" diagram is a potential entry ramp. Each point leads to the discovery of greater meaning and purpose. There is no "right" or "wrong" place to enter. Any point in outer the ring can take you to any point on the inner ring. Enter wherever you find your connection or resonance.

CYCLE OF INSPIRATION AND PERSONAL FULFILLMENT

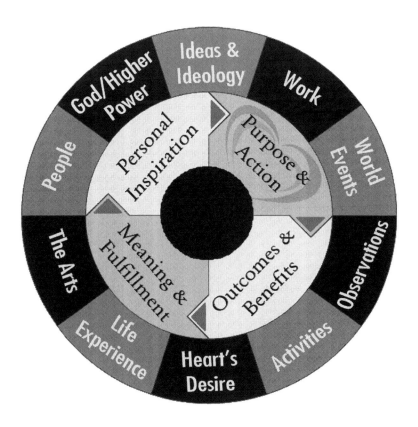

To illustrate the process, we will begin by exploring the source of nspiration on the outer ring, at the top of the cycle.

The Outer Circle: Sources of Inspiration

The outer ring represents sources of inspiration. These include but are not limited to:

- Ideas and Ideology
- Work
- World Events
- Observations
- Activities

- Your Heart's Desire
- Life Experiences
- The Arts
- People
- God or Higher Power

Of course, there are many other sources that can inspire us. What has inspired you?

What is inspiration, exactly, and why does it matter? The word inspiration originally referred to the spiritual breath, coupled with motion or direction, sparking initiative to do something or go someplace. Our definition is very similar. We think of inspiration as an energetic feeling triggered when your mind and emotions are prompted to act and create. Inspiration excites and energizes you about a vision or concept and spurs you to action. More spiritual definitions focus on inspiration as a "divine influence" leading to revelation and influential acts.

The essence of inspiration is that it drives us in some way, and it can be triggered by almost anything:

- A deeply beautiful sunset
- The story of a young person's bravery in the face of chronic illness
- A compelling story about the difference someone made in the lives of others
- Readings from spiritual texts or poetry
- An idea from a friend or family member
- A news story about a desperate situation in your community
- A thrilling theatrical or musical performance

Inspiration only becomes meaningful, however, when it is translated

> "Don't ask what the world needs. Ask what makes you come alive, and go do it. Because what the world needs is people who have come alive."
> — Howard Thurman

into significant action. Taking action creates value and propels your purpose, which ultimately can add fulfillment to your life.

Many people have a vision of a world that is whole: enough food, drink, and shelter for everyone, kindness as the foundation for all human behavior, people working together in camaraderie and joy.

Each religious tradition recognizes this vision in its own way. Christianity recognizes the Messianic Era. Hinduism embraces the concept of the soul ascending to a perfect place. Judaism, in its daily prayers, recites that the soul is pure. Likewise, as individuals, we may have a desire to make this planet a better place, one that better reflects our inner vision of wholeness.

These moments of inspiration and their resulting actions give us a sense of meaning and purpose, while simultaneously creating wholeness in the world. You are now beginning (or continuing) your life as a heartisan. And so the cycle continues.

Inspiration can occur organically, slowly evolving over time through an accumulation of experiences, exposure to ideas, education, parental influences, or any combination of factors. It may not happen in a single moment, but could potentially result from many sources that together inspire you over time, perhaps without you even realizing it until that "ah-ha" moment occurs. Once again, we stress that there is no right or wrong way to be inspired. Each of us has our own path.

The Inner Circle

The inner ring represents the results of acting on your inspiration. These include but are not limited to:

- Personal Inspiration
- Purpose & Action
- Outcomes/Benefits
- Personal Meaning and Fulfillment

Personal Inspiration

Personal revelation or epiphany, combined with your motivation to act, constitutes your personal inspiration. Your personal inspiration and how you act on it will eventually determine your identity. As you pursue your source of inspiration, the answer to the questions, "Who am I" and "Where am I?" will become clearer. Your inspiration will help create your vision, whether for you personally, for your family, an organization, your community, the nation, or for the world at large. You are the designer and the navigator – you chart the course.

Inspiration that impels us to improve something or take action has value; otherwise, it is just a good feeling, idea, or unrealized desire. Unrealized desires lead to "if onlys."

Purpose

Inspiration alone is not enough; it is only the beginning. Inspiration without action leads nowhere. Use your inspiration to help define your purpose. You might write it down or discuss it with others. As you consider your inspiration and gather input from others, you will likely refine and crystallize your purpose, and become adept at communicating about it quite easily.

You may find that you wish to pursue more than one purpose. That's a great ambition. However, we suggest that you focus on just one purpose to get the ball rolling, especially if you are new at this personal development work. Once you've become clearly focused on one purpose, you may choose to add others, as appropriate. For those with an already clearly defined purpose who wish to expand it, the sky's the limit.

Action

Achieving one's purpose requires action. To be most effective, we suggest creating and following a plan. First, though, you should develop measurable and realistic goals for achieving your purpose over a certain period of time. The goals may be immediate, set to take place in the next few weeks or even within the next couple of days! Or they may be more long-term, requiring several years to achieve.

Take the story of Anna. She was born prematurely, weighing only 3.5 pounds. With tiny, immature lungs, she spent her first year on a heart-respiration monitor that alerted her parents if she stopped breathing. As Anna grew up and learned about her struggles as an infant, she was drawn to work with babies in similar situations. In high school, she volunteered at the local hospital on Saturdays, specifically requesting to help care for the "preemies." She nurtured very sick babies, talked with worried parents, and escorted infants to their parents' cars when they were released. Inspired by her volunteer experience, she now intends to become a neonatologist.

Anna found a purpose, developed a vision, and took action. She jokes that she is a movie star, captured in hundreds of home movies taken by parents recording their babies' departures from the hospital. And Anna is fine with the fact that, years later, when the families watch the video, most will have forgotten who she was and what she did. She will remember, and the fulfillment she experienced will continue to glow within her.

> The heart is the connector between purpose and action, because purpose without action has no value.

As you begin to achieve your goals, you will set new ones to further advance your efforts. This process of planning and action can also help you engage others to join you and identify the roles each of them will play as you move your purpose forward.

Action Defining Purpose

Perhaps you haven't yet found your purpose. A great way to begin is by taking action – either more of the actions you are already taking or through involvement in new activities with new people. The more exposed you become to work already in progress, the more likely you are to find the inspiration you seek. If your passion is to make award-winning documentaries, for example, find a way to spend time with documentarians who are already making excellent films. Your activities, conversations, and the new people you meet will all be part of an incubation process that will ultimately reach fruition. You may find that you need to practice patience and reflection until that flicker of inspiration ignites for you. By taking action, you will eventually find one or more arenas that fulfill you.

The Heart

The heart is the connector between purpose and action, because purpose without action has no value. Actions drive purpose. Purpose and action work together synergistically. In tandem, they generate a much greater impact than either could without the other. While your actions may help you define your purpose, your purpose will also drive your actions.

This relationship is well illustrated in Dov Vogel's experience as a hospital clown. His daughter recognized immediately that clowning fit Dov's personality, so he took the course and jumped in. His actions and subsequent experience affirmed his choice. Serving as a hospital clown became his purpose and also enhanced his life. Dov's enthusiasm was truly contagious; the more he clowned, the more fulfilled he felt, and the happier – and perhaps more inspired were the people whose lives he touched.

Outcomes and Benefits

Inspiration not just a starting place; it can sometimes be a result. A smile, a hug, others' joy, tears of happiness, seeing a project completed, and helping others are outcomes and benefits that flow from your work, and they may be your greatest reward. There may be nothing more gratifying than seeing how your efforts make a difference for a person or a community, and that result can reinforce your efforts and inspire you to continue to live a purpose-infused life. Dov was able to see the impact of his clowning immediately. In other cases, however – especially those that focus on broader issues or community needs – the impact may take more time to become apparent.

As you begin to see the results, benefits, and impact of your work, you will recognize the transformational power of your purpose in the world, not only in filling your life with meaning and satisfaction, but in affecting the lives of so many others. The experience of counselors at Camp Swift illustrates this well. The youth counselors watch the expressions on the campers' faces as they enjoy daily activities and participate in programs designed to instill values related to improving their grades, staying in school, avoiding gang involvement, helping others, and simply doing the right thing. The most remarkable outcome is that they see new possibilities for their future.

The impact of their work is profound for many of the Camp Swift counselors. In just a few days, they witness the transformation of angry, undisciplined children into kids who have released their troubles and finally feel free to be themselves. They see the effect they have on children only a few years younger who have not enjoyed the same privileges they have generally taken for granted. As a result, many teen counselors have gone on to develop a deep passion for social justice activities and giving back. Some have remained connected to Camp Swift as adults. Others have started their own small foundations, with lifelong commitments to making a difference in their communities – as volunteers or as professionals in nonprofit organizations.

A former Camp Swift camper recently wrote this letter:

I grew up in South Phoenix, Arizona. I moved many times and was surrounded by gangs and drugs. I was an A student and was an athlete in school, but to survive the tough surroundings, joining a gang provided protection and friends. Soon, I learned that it was really a bad idea, but it was too late. As things got worse, I looked for an outlet and it all started with Camp Swift!

I went with two of my gang friends and it showed us there was a better life out there. People actually cared for us and truly wanted better for me and my friends. The police officer at my school sent us and it changed my life. My experience was a camping trip and we built tents, went fishing, and made s'mores. They brought people from the zoo to showcase some animals! We played team sports and had mixers to meet other kids. But most of all, my counselor got to know me and helped me with my situation.

I escaped my old gang alive and started a new life! I went on to be accepted to the Naval Academy and got offers to the Berkeley School of Music. I graduated from Thunderbird High School with honors and scholarships! Camp Swift truly changed my life!

Camp Swift's impact extends even further than the campers and the counselors, inspiring many others who have never visited the camp. These include the campers' teachers, the counselors' younger siblings, and friends and families of both. Like that proverbial rock tossed into a pond, the ripple effects continue far beyond what the eye can see in the moment.

Personal Meaning and Fulfillment

Sometimes we are able to see obvious results as we work toward our purpose. Other times, outcomes may be more subtle, perhaps taking many years before we see results. Regardless of our ability to witness tangible results, we gain personal satisfaction through our purpose-focused activities, whether they involve volunteering, philanthropy, athletics, business, artistic endeavors, professional functions, or other undertakings that create value. Harvard Business School professor Howard Stevenson and senior research fellow Laura Nash, authors of *Four Keys of Enduring Success: How High Achievers Win*, found through their research on enduring success that satisfaction comes more from the act of achieving than from the actual accomplishment. This point is significant in a world that often measures success by our accomplishments. It is important to understand that the endeavor itself creates our feelings of fulfillment.

Matthew Kelly, author of *Perfectly Yourself: 9 Lessons for Enduring Happiness*, suggests that self-fulfillment stems from the combination of achievement and happiness. He makes a distinction between momentary happiness – like something you might experience at a celebration – and enduring happiness. He fo-

INNER QUEST
What would be personally fulfilling for you?

OUTER QUEST
What meaningful action could you take to create it?

cuses, as we do, on the enduring aspects. Happiness and fulfillment are woven into the fiber of your being and serve as anchors in good times and bad. Among Kelly's lessons for enduring happiness are:

- Celebrate your progress.
- Just do the next right thing.
- Put character first.
- Live what you believe.

In the chapters that follow, we explore the elements of enduring success and happiness, along with other factors we consider essential for the journey toward living a fulfilling and purposeful life.

Personal fulfillment is that all-over, deep-inside good feeling we get when we invest ourselves in an effort that creates value. We feel it when we do something good for ourselves, like maintaining our commitment to an exercise program. The feeling becomes even larger, however, when we go outside ourselves. Investing in a team effort and contributing to the greater good instantly taps into something bigger than we are, and the rewards are exponentially richer.

Coming Full Circle

As you become more deeply invested in your purpose, new ideas and more profound inspiration may result, strengthening your dedication to your purpose, which may lead to an even greater sense of personal fulfillment.

Sometimes a small gesture, a simple act of kindness, or allowing yourself to trust an unlikely person can lead to the discovery of a deeper purpose that profoundly impacts your life. Action can lead to purpose and personal fulfillment, just as purpose can lead to action.

The Sages of Judaism say that the one who gives of herself gains much more than she gives. While the recipient is always grateful, the giver often feels like she received the bigger gift. This is the magic of personal fulfillment. It is fuel for the next leg of the journey.

Inspiration for Others

One of the greatest compliments is knowing that your actions have inspired others to similar movement. Others may join your efforts, carry on your work with you and/or after you, or they may be otherwise inspired because your example helped them define their own purpose. Regardless of what that inspiration looks like, it is immensely gratifying to know you have ignited a spark in someone else. It is one of the ways your legacy lives on.

Epiphanies – sudden or unexpected insights or realizations – may be spiritual in nature. They might spring from a near-death experience or recovery from a serious operation or illness, or they could simply be ah-has as you marvel at the wonder of the universe or contemplate the miracle of life and nature. And, of course, inspiration can also come as a result of your own good deeds or creative outlets. Regardless of the source, these serve as entry points on your journey to a purpose-enhanced life. The key, of course, is to act on them, so that you can enrich your life and the lives of others.

NAVIGATIONAL POINTS

- You can begin anywhere. The key is to start ... there is no right or wrong way.
- Inspiration and the pursuit of your purpose can come from a single event, an ah-ha moment, or an experience of the heart. They can also evolve from cumulative life experiences.
- You need not wait for inspiration to spark you; action is a great trigger for inspiration.
- Personal inspiration and commitment may deepen with engagement.

- Purpose and action are synergistic, and at the heart of the process of finding fulfillment.
- Turn your inspiration into something tangible by defining your purpose, taking action, setting goals, and working toward those goals.
- Your inspiration and your pursuit of it can engage and inspire others.
- You can develop your inspiration into a life of purpose that gives you great meaning.

APPLYING THE CONCEPTS TO YOUR LIFE

1. What are, have been, or could be sources of inspiration for you?

2. What causes or unmet needs do you have a passion for or would you like to explore as possible LifePath destinations?

3. What are some possible first steps – or next steps – toward turning this cause into a life purpose? These might include people to contact, researching organizations and agencies involved in this work, or just jotting down some ideas.

Chapter 4

Values: You Are What You Value

Becoming rooted

Being true to yourself

Applying a guiding framework to decisions and actions

The Courage of Convictions:
M. Zuhdi Jasser and the American Islamic Forum for Democracy

"I hope it was not Muslims who did this." This was the initial reaction of several members of the Phoenix Muslim community, before we knew who was responsible for the 9/11 terrorist attacks on the World Trade Center towers in New York and the Pentagon in Washington, D.C., as another plane crashed in rural Pennsylvania. When the Islamic terrorist organization Al Queda claimed responsibility, an emotional tsunami hit. It was as if this quiet group of Muslims living in the Arizona desert, who had been participating in a monthly meeting with members of the Jewish community with a goal of fostering mutual understanding and improved relations, had been personally attacked.

It did not take long for other ramifications to echo, as well. The Muslims began to be pelted with questions and feel the wariness expressed by non-Muslim friends and colleagues; their children were taunted in school and became isolated; and a general distrust by people in the broader community descended upon them as a group. They became afraid, for perhaps the first time, in their adopted or native country. As one member of the Muslim group said, "This could be one of the worst things ever to happen to the Muslim community in the United States."

Steve met Zuhdi Jasser in 2000, when both were members of this Jewish-Muslim discussion group, later named "Children of Abraham." The group was formed by the rabbi and members of Steve's synagogue and a group of Muslim professionals and businesspeople. Both groups were understandably wary of each other at first. "Can we trust them? Do they have a hidden agenda? Will we like them? Will they like us? Will we have anything in common?"

> It takes personal courage and the courage of your convictions to stand up for what you believe, especially when others vehemently oppose your position.

Conversation during the first couple of meetings was confined to safe topics, simply getting to know one other as people. Then, the members of the group decided to spend the next few monthly meetings learning about each others' religions and traditions. Discussion of politics, the Middle East, and other sensitive subjects was forbidden. And then 9/11 happened.

The members of the two groups phoned each other, commiserating in the tragedy. All were aware that beyond the international crisis the attacks generated, these horrific events could destroy the delicate, still-forming friendships and trust that had been so carefully nurtured. Fortunately, empathy and deeper understanding prevailed, as deep rifts within the Islamic community became dramatically apparent.

Reactions varied widely within the broader American Muslim community. Some tried to rationalize the terrorist attacks. Others became radicalized – or further radicalized – as the United States came to terms with the new threat. Still others blamed Israel, or claimed it was a conspiracy against Islam. The Muslim community, never fully integrated, became even further isolated.

Zuhdi Jasser's response was dramatically and significantly different from that of most American Muslims. He drew on the deeply embedded values he had been taught by his parents, Muslim-Syrian immigrants to the United States. These values and their example became the nexus of Zuhdi's inspiration. He never saw a conflict between God, Islam, his country, and taking a stand to do what he felt was right.

It takes personal courage and the courage of your convictions to stand up for what you believe, especially when many others vehemently oppose your position. Taking a stand and holding fast to it when powerful people oppose you requires a strong sense of values and commitment, particularly when many others who may support you do so only silently, fearful of the risk involved. Zuhdi Jasser had stepped into precisely this vortex.

Individual freedom, compassion, integrity, intellectual honesty, pluralism, justice, and doing no harm form the tapestry of Zuhdi's values and principles. They are an integrated set of values that guide his day-to-day and long-term behavior. Individual freedom is his highest value. He is also points out that the word compassion begins with "compass" – a navigational tool. His personal compass is anchored in the sacred texts of the Qur'an.

Zuhdi lives out his convictions in many arenas. He is a patriotic American, a devout and moderate Muslim, and a highly regarded physician. He was a U.S. Naval doctor and is a past president of the Arizona Medical Association. He also is a shining example of a person who lives by his principles and values, sometimes at significant personal sacrifice.

One of the strongest voices in the American Muslim community against radical Islam, Zuhdi founded and still chairs the American Islamic Forum for Democracy (AIFD), a group created post-9/11. Its mission is to "build the future of Islam though liberty and freedom – with separation of mosque and state." This is the crystallization of his inspiration.

Always an activist, Zuhdi found his circle of Muslim friends shrinking after 9/11, as his voice became stronger and more prominent. He has been threatened with libel suits, among other things, by fellow Muslims for advocating his beliefs. And, yet, a core Islamic principle propels him forward. He explains that he and all of us "are bestowed with gifts and challenges, and on Judgment Day, God will judge us, not in comparison to others, but on whether we used our abilities and gifts to maximal capacity." He asks, "If I don't do it, who will? Who can?"

Zuhdi believes there is a huge need to embed the ideas and values he is championing into Muslim consciousness. He realizes, however, that this is an incremental process, and the pieces will gradually build on each other until, ultimately, significant breakthroughs occur.

Zuhdi sees an analogy between his striving and the American Civil Rights Movement. He asks everyone associated with AIFD to watch *The Great Debaters*, a movie set in the Jim Crow era American South at Wiley College, an historically African-American university in Marshall, Texas. The debate coach, Melvin Tolson, portrayed in the movie by Denzel Washington, seeks excellence, accomplishment, and recognition for his team. Tolson's push pays off as Wiley debates and wins against larger, more prestigious black and white colleges. In the movie, Tolson seeks and receives an unprecedented invitation for the Wiley Debate Team to debate the reigning national champion, Harvard. (In reality, it was the University of Southern California.) Wiley wins the debate in front of a packed auditorium, and goes undefeated for ten years.

Zuhdi makes the point that all of this occurred approximately twenty-five years before the American Civil Rights Movement picked up steam under the leadership of Martin Luther King, Jr. and thirty years before President Johnson signed the Civil Rights Act of 1964. Yet the achievements of the Wiley Debate Team served as a significant demarcation, one of many accomplishments that formed the foundation for the vigorous Civil Rights Movement to come. Zuhdi sees his work and mission in the same vein.

As a physician, Zuhdi also draws medical analogies. He sees the ideological problems in the Muslim community as a disease, a cancer that desperately needs to be treated. He believes the community must stop the smoking that exacerbates the disease, or it really will find itself in need of emergency resuscitation. Both the epidemic and the actions that cause it must be addressed in order for effective change to take hold. Medical ethics dictate that if a physician has the ability to solve a problem, he or she must take the appropriate actions to do so. Zuhdi feels that his medical obligations are reinforced by his religious commitments. It is his devotional responsibility to act on behalf of Islam. He cites an Islamic article of faith: "If you find an issue based on principles that you do not address, you will be judged negatively on Judgment Day."

Zuhdi's love of Islam and his love of medicine complement and reinforce each other. He says, "Patients need to feel that I love them as human beings before they will listen to me. I even hug my patients." They feel his compassion. He feels the same is true for his religion, and he almost always expresses his love of Islam in interviews and speeches. His faith is the reason he does what he does.

But he is not an idealist. Zuhdi recognizes the tremendous resistance he faces from the Muslim community and the outsized influence of radicals; he is trying to push a huge boulder up a steep hill. However, unlike the mythological character Sisyphus, Zuhdi is exerting his energy on a meaningful task. And although Zuhdi feels there is even more to be done now than when he began his work, this journey must continue. As the problem appears to be significantly worsening, Zuhdi is all the more motivated.

He explains that Muslims are obligated to come together to preserve their community. This concept is often used by radical Islamists to rationalize their actions. Its origins can be traced back to the time when Muslims were a minority. Today, Zuhdi explains, this concept is outmoded, especially in countries where

Muslims are a majority, and in western countries like the United States, where minority rights are protected. Zuhdi feels his obligation is to preserve his community, which he defines as the nation in which he lives and the values it represents.

Additionally, Zuhdi believes that Muslims and other minority groups in the United States and around the world must advocate the same causes they would advance if they were the majority. They must be transparent and act with integrity, intellectual honesty, and good faith, without being hypocritical or duplicitous.

What keeps Zuhdi going? His children are growing up, and his efforts are also for them. He wants them to live in a world that his work has helped improve. He feels strongly that his belief and understanding of Islam are correct and just, and that political Islam is misguided: religious law should never be a part of government. Zuhdi's standard is the United States Constitution. He believes that God is the center of each individual, not of society. One Western blessing Zuhdi cherishes is the freedom of worship. America gives him that freedom, which makes everything else possible.

Zuhdi tells of a time when he spoke to a group of mostly Muslim students at Stanford University. Students objected to the principles and values of his message. In this situation, he focused on engaging the people he wanted to transform. He drew three circles on the board with the words "Islam," "individual freedom," and "God" in them. He then explained that these students had been taught about Islam by their parents, reminding them that it is a way of life, not a concept conferred on them by government. "If we accept that God is inside us, that God is our personal center, then all we need is the individual freedom, such as that made possible in Western societies, to make God real in our lives," Zuhdi explained to this student group and other Muslim assemblies. "Without that liberty, we cannot follow Islam freely. Our choices become limited. The three components must work together for Islam to truly flourish and be expressed meaningfully, individualistically, and constructively."

As some of the students understood, followed, and accepted his logic, Zuhdi felt progress. He sensed he was making an impression and altering their mindset about Islam and the society in which they lived. He sees this as one step needed to shift Islam to a different path. Zuhdi sees the potential for these small shifts to accumulate, eventually reaching the point where a new pathway becomes the norm.

For more information about the American Islamic Forum for Democracy, visit aifdemocracy.org.

The Value of Values

Our values reflect the choices we make, consciously or unconsciously, about how we live our lives. They are frequently unarticulated, yet we always demonstrate them in our behavior patterns and decisions. Examples of values include integrity, generosity, kindness, compassion, respect, loyalty, service, fairness, humility, giving back, and the courage of convictions. Our values are defined by the sum of our choices and actions,

> If you want to create a meaningful life for yourself, one that fulfills you each day, you must first know what is important to you.

rather than what we say or believe them to be. It is very important, and at times challenging, to align our stated values with our actions. We may say something is important to us, while our actions tell a different story. For example, we may claim we value kindness, but turn around and make hurtful comments or act more inconsiderately than we realize. Aligning our values with our actions is a daily, even moment-to-moment, process.

If we do not live out the values we claim, others can only guess about the things that are important to us. We leave them to form assumptions and conclusions based on the behaviors they observe. In a sense, our values are largely defined by the perceptions of others. If you go the extra mile for someone, reach out to help a colleague, or treat others with grace and a good heart, people may describe you as kind; however, if you are short-tempered, self-centered, impatient, or hurtful to others, they would not view you as someone who demonstrates the value of kindness. We strengthen our self-integrity when we align our actions with our stated values.

If you want to create a meaningful life for yourself, one that fulfills you each day, you must first know what is important to you. It is critical that you assess your values and then live by them, because in living our values, we add meaning to our lives. The active and consistent demonstration of our values has positive consequences: others will trust us and want to invest in our vision and work, enabling us to achieve greater results. Much of our fulfillment and meaning in life comes from what we do with, for, and through others. Therefore, the more genuinely we reflect our values, the more meaning and purpose we may ultimately find.

Here's an example of the ripple effects created by living our values:

- **My personal value:** I consistently demonstrate the value of integrity.
- **My behavioral commitment:** I demonstrate integrity in my interactions with others, my decisions and choices, my work, and how I handle routine and challenging situations. I demonstrate integrity through honesty, ethical decisions and actions, and keeping my commitments.
- **The possible impact of these value-based behaviors:**

  For others: They have trust and confidence in me and are willing to reciprocate integrity in their actions.

  For me: I gain personal fulfillment from being true to myself and living my values, develop stronger personal and business relationships and referrals, and easily gain commitments from others.

  Broader impact: I am seen as a role model, and I influence others' behavior.

To make this real for yourself, think about someone you admire and respect. Identify the personal characteristics they exhibit that cause you to respect them. These are the values they embody. Now consider the steps above:

- What would you say is his or her personal commitment?
- What impact does this have on others? (Think of the impact it has on you.)
- What impact does their personal commitment have on them?
- What broader impact(s) are you aware of?

This exercise will help you appreciate the importance of identifying your values and then living by them, as well as demonstrating how they play a significant role in achieving your goals and visions. Personal values are characteristics you can control and choose to use as guides for living; therein lies their power.

Flourishing as a Heartisan: Fulfilling Your Purpose on a Busy Schedule

Zuhdi Jasser's project is ambitious and requires a huge time commitment. If you can devote that much time and energy to your purpose, by all means, go for it! Many of us, however, have very busy lives that may include family and work obligations. The great news is that you can exemplify the concepts in this chapter in a way that works for you, perhaps with just "bite-size" pieces of time. Here's an example:

Barbara prizes justice as a value. Inspired by Dennis Fritz's book, *Journey Toward Justice*, she realized there are many such stories about wrongful convictions and people who have been exonerated. Her interest in justice led her to look for a way to help these people clear their names publicly. She started a blog where they can tell their stories, including how they reintegrated themselves back into society.

Like Barbara, Zuhdi Jasser's values are very clear, and they guide his everyday actions, both as a physician and in the stands he has taken within the Muslim community. Personal values must link with our causes and define our personal integrity. If we value justice, we must stand for it. If we value integrity, we must do what is morally right and honest. Actively demonstrating our values helps guard against their erosion. Barbara values justice and actively works to help others achieve it. Zuhdi Jasser repeatedly stands up for what he believes is right, even at some personal risk. He takes the initiative to challenge terrorist acts and situations emanating from Islam that he believes are morally wrong. His values define him as a person of principle.

Over time, your values may change or deepen. We grow in wisdom as a result of our life experiences and mistakes. As we accumulate experiences and learn from them, our focus and priorities may change, and with them the values we consider most important. We may deliberately refine them; we may also become more aware of inconsistencies between our values and our actions. The tough part is translating the character changes we desire into actual, consistent behavior patterns. Our current habits may be so embedded, occurring so automatically, that changing them will require a continual conscious effort and discipline, until they, too, become natural for us.

People often feel stuck in old habits and frustrated when they have difficulty breaking free of them. We explore the challenge of altering and replacing long-standing behavior patterns with others that better reflect your desired values in Chapter 11, "Passion to Action to Fruition."

> "Persons with weight of character carry, like planets, their atmosphere along with them in their orbits."
> — Thomas Hardy

Key Questions to Consider

- By which values do I want to live and define my life?
- What are my values now, as reflected by the sum of my actions?
- How aligned are my desired values with my actual behaviors and decisions? Where do I need to realign my actions with my values?
- How do I bring my values and actions into alignment?

Stated values become true values when they are aligned with your behavior, and as you embody and live them over time.

SAMPLE VALUES AND DEFINITIONS

Below are a few sample values. *A more complete list can be found at FindFulfillFlourish.com by clicking on Book & Tools. Follow the Tools drop-down menu.*

Value	Definition
Community	Strengthening the bonds and cohesiveness between and among people living in the same area or who are members of a group or organization.
Compassion	Demonstrating the desire to alleviate sorrow or suffering; showing tenderness and mercy; being good-hearted.
Fairness	Making decisions and acting in ways free from bias, prejudice or self-interest; judging based on factual information and consistent standards.
Fun/Joy	Injecting amusement, playfulness, happiness, pleasure, or delight into activities and situations.
Hard Work/Self-Discipline	Devoting the time and effort to effectively and thoroughly complete tasks and achieve goals; exercising control over one's actions and establishing priorities to fulfill assignments and commitments in a timely and effective manner.

Teamwork	Acting together cooperatively and collaboratively with others in a group for a common purpose.
Trustworthiness	Demonstrating, through words and actions, that others can confidently rely on your integrity, motivations, competence, and promises.

What are some other values you embody or aspire to?

If you would like help in identifying or prioritizing your top values, visit FindFulfill-Flourish.com. Log in using Coupon Code GBC3MN24 to become a member, which will also provide you access to the entire website. Then click on Find Your Purpose: Guiding Values Exercise. It's an engaging activity, and it's free.

When we define and commit to our personal values, they will guide our lives. They are especially helpful when we face challenging or ambiguous situations or have tough decisions to make. Each time our actions are consistent with our stated values, we become more true to ourselves, reinforce our self-integrity, generate self-respect, and develop genuine pride in who we are and how we behave. The opposite is true as well: when we stray from our values, we lose credibility with ourselves and with others. In tough situations, or when something significant is at stake, it may seem easier to cut integrity corners or make excuses.

INNER QUEST
What are your top 5 values?

OUTER QUEST
How do you demonstrate them?

Think of times when you may have chosen expediency and compromised your values for one reason or another. It may have been an innocent or unimportant issue, but nonetheless, you sacrificed your integrity – even if you were the only one who knew. These instances diminish us and the meaning we wish to create for our lives.

To break this down a bit further, we can examine a statement from Stephen R. Covey, author of *The 7 Habits of Highly Effective People*: "You can't talk your way out of problems you behaved your way into." The circumstances we create with our actions cannot be undone with a few words here or there. In contrast, however, Covey's son, Stephen M. R. Covey adds in his book, *The Speed of Trust*, "You can behave yourself out of a problem you behaved your way into." This is important to remember: the actions we take can clean up past mistakes, even severe ones. The Coveys' point, like ours, is that lapses in integrity and other values can be resolved, but only through actions that bring your behavior and values into alignment. This is the moment when values become authentic

What drives a departure from our stated values and the childhood lessons we once believed were important? It varies from person to person. Causes may emanate from lack, fear, or anxiety. We may worry that we won't have enough, that we won't get ahead, or that we won't be liked. Other reasons may include resentment due to a feeling of injustice, exploitation, unfair or insensitive treatment, being overlooked or ignored, and other real or perceived slights.

The unfortunate irony is that, in many cases, when we behave in ways that depart from our values, we often get the result we feared: when we take more than is ours, we may be punished or offered fewer opportunities. When we break rules or behave unethically, we may become excluded from business, professional, and recreational options. Our actions have consequences, even if they are not immediately apparent. We eventually reap what we sow.

We may rationalize our actions by telling ourselves that our lapses are small or insignificant. Yet they send a big message. Small breaches of trust, honesty, and insensitivity matter more than we think.

It may be a big challenge to rise above your anxieties or anger for your own benefit, as well as for the greater good. Yet overcoming these negative emotions, to whatever degree possible, is an important key to creating a fulfilling life rooted in your values. Living your values even when it is most difficult has its own rewards, and you may be amazed by how it is reciprocated – perhaps when you least expect it or when you most need it. Often, the more we give away, the more we receive.

As William Shakespeare wrote in *Hamlet*, "This above all: to thine own self be true, and it must follow, as the night the day, thou canst not then be false to any man." Or as Zuhdi Jasser said so well, if he were not living his values and advocating for his beliefs, he would "be living a façade." It may take extraordinary courage to be true to yourself – to your own values, ethics, and beliefs – during challenging situations or when much is at stake. This kind of courage will define you as a principled and respected individual. More importantly, it is the essence of self-integrity and self-respect.

When we skirt our values, we erode our own integrity and the principles we feel important enough to instill in our children. We lose the opportunity to be positive role models and we work at cross-purposes with the future we desire to create. We must emulate our vision of the future through our own actions in the present.

In doing so, we may find that such behavior is contagious. Our kids may catch it, as may our colleagues and coworkers, friends, family, acquaintances, and indeed our whole community. The impact we have may be far greater than we realize.

Sometimes we get caught up in our own emotional responses to people or situations, and as a result, we make excuses for violating our values. We may say to ourselves, "It's okay, because he did it to me first." Or we may rationalize these violations because "everyone else is doing it," even though we know that does not really justify our behavior. We all occasionally see behavior that is out of integrity in our dearest role models: parents, teachers, organizational and political leaders, even clergy – people from whom we expect more.

Sometimes, because these individuals have so much influence in our lives, we begin to model their undesirable behaviors. It is almost as if they have unconsciously transferred their breach in values to us. People in positions of authority have a particular responsibility to model their values because of their significant impact and influence on others. When authority figures consistently demonstrate their values, both publicly and privately, they can become a powerful force for good, with enormous ripple effects.

Regardless of the reason, as soon as we become aware that we have breached our values, we must restore them. In the process of returning to our true values, we may have some ground to make up. This may feel confusing at first, make us less competitive, lead to frustration, or necessitate sacrificing something we want, yet these losses are insignificant compared to the loss of personal integrity we will experience if we let our values go unrestored. Some say that giving into these temptations is akin to "selling your soul."

The choice begins with you. You have incredible power to realize your vision, your purpose, and your goals, but you must first be the person you want your world to reflect and model.

Our values may occasionally conflict. An example might be the decision about whether to give upsetting news to someone who is terminally ill and nearing death. Should you be honest or compassionate when asked about the situation? Which is more important? To help guide difficult choices like these, you may wish to identify a driving value for yourself, which will help you prioritize the two conflicting values.

CYCLE OF INSPIRATION AND PERSONAL FULFILLMENT

The "Cycle of Inspiration and Personal Fulfillment" revolves around an individual's core values. One's values are integral to all parts of the cycle. Our day-to-day values reflect who we are and who we need to be to create the future we desire for ourselves and others. In living these values, we make ourselves role models for others to emulate.

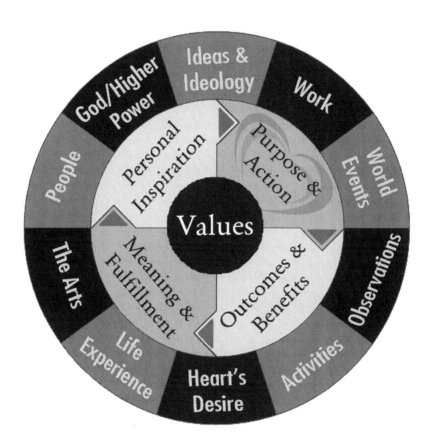

Values can take many forms. They anchor us to our core beliefs. They provide a guiding framework for how we treat others, make decisions, and take action. They form a critical part of our identity, as well as how others see us and whether they trust us. They provide the foundation for who we are as human beings. Solidifying our values is an important stage in finding fulfillment in life. Exercises in the next section of this chapter will help you identify your personal values, reflect on your consistency in living them, and take steps to strengthen them.

NAVIGATIONAL POINTS

- Your true values are demonstrated by your collective choices and actions, which may differ from what you proclaim them to be. You enhance your self-integrity when you align your behaviors with your stated values, strengthening your identity.

- Living your values adds meaning to your life and makes you a positive role model for others.

- Your values guide the decisions you make about how you live | your life.

- Living your values when there may be more expedient ways of achieving goals takes courage and strength of character.

- Remember to live out life's early lessons.

- Values are about HOW you choose to live your life.

APPLYING THE CONCEPTS TO YOUR LIFE

1. List some actions or decisions you feel good about.
   - What do these actions and decisions say about you?
   - What values do they demonstrate?
   - What values might others say these actions reflect?

2. List some actions or decisions you regret.
   - What do these actions and decisions say about you?
   - What values do they demonstrate?
   - What values might others say these actions reflect?

Please visit FindFulfillFlourish.com and log in using Coupon Code GBC3MN24. Click on Book & Tools for an extension of this exercise. You may also access the Guiding Values Exercise from the Find Your Purpose tab.

Chapter 5

Inspired Direction:
Purpose, Vision, and Action

Embracing a purpose

Creating a vision

Putting your purpose in motion

A Society Where Everyone Counts:
Denise D. Resnik and the Southwest Autism Research & Resource Center

Denise loved Saturdays – that was the day she took her weekly hike with her husband and two beautiful children, Allyson and Matthew. The whole family looked forward to their Saturday ritual all week long. Enchanted by the beautiful, sunny Phoenix weather and the first blossoms of spring, Denise remembers this particularly happy day. Little did she know that while the family was enjoying cactus blooms and each others' company, their house was filling with water. They would come home to a mammoth flood, because her son, Matthew, had stuffed an entire roll of toilet paper into the bowl before they'd left the house. Matthew was not playing a practical joke, nor was he a mean-spirited child. He simply did not understand the consequences of many of his actions. Matthew has autism.

Years have passed since Denise and her husband spent countless hours mopping up the many floods that overtook their home. Matthew is now 18 and attends a public high school. Highlights of his school day include computer class, chorus, PE, and culinary arts. His mom says of him, "He is the hardest working teenager I know. He helps extensively with all kinds of chores around the house, and he's also my weekend warrior, enjoying the many hikes, bicycle trips, and yoga sessions we do together." Matthew also takes special education classes with a full-time aide supporting him, and holds two volunteer jobs, one at the high school and the other at the public library. Libraries are some of Matthew's favorite places; he loves books, letters, numbers, and order.

As a child with an autism spectrum disorder, Matthew's incredible progress did not come quickly or easily. Denise wanted to create a vision for her son that was different from the one painted by the diagnosing physician who told her to "love and accept Matthew, and plan to institutionalize him, because there's little hope for children with autism." This has been Denise's commitment since Matthew was two years old, when he was diagnosed. She learned all she could about this complex, confusing disorder and researched ways for her son and others like him to experience full lives as part of communities that respect and value their unique talents and differences.

Denise's vision was ambitious, and some might say unrealistic. Working toward it became a full-time job, in addition to running her own marketing and public relations firm. In 1997, Denise cofounded and launched the Southwest Autism Research & Resource Center (SARRC). This nonprofit organization is dedicated to "advancing research discoveries and supporting individuals with autism and their families throughout their lifetimes." With seemingly boundless energy, Denise juggled all of these responsibilities, in addition to her role as wife and mother of two.

When describing how she got started, Denise recalls her grade school and high school days. "The idea of helping others was always part of my life. My sister, who is just seventeen months older and my very best friend, was diagnosed with diabetes at the age of ten. My mother cofounded the Arizona Diabetes Association and did other volunteer work, as well. Both she and my dad were committed to many causes, so I was surrounded by volunteerism. It was part of our dinner table discussions and after-school and weekend activities. It brought us together as a family and has kept us together through the years. In high school, I organized events to raise money for the diabetes association. I was committed to helping my sister and others similarly affected.

"When I discovered that Matthew was not like other children, I was committed to doing everything possible, and then some, to understand his challenges and help him. We initially noticed things were different after his first birthday. We thought he might be going deaf, because he stopped responding to his name and lost his first few very precious words." Deafness was quickly ruled out by doctors. By the time Matthew was two, Denise, and her husband, Rob, learned that their son had autism. At that time, autism was diagnosed in one out of ten thousand children in the U.S.; today it is diagnosed in one in ten.

> Denise had a vision for her son. While she had no idea what he was capable of, she wanted to help him fulfill his potential. And perhaps, while unaware of it, Denise was developing her own life purpose at the same time.

Denise didn't accept the diagnosis at face value. She saw brightness in Matthew's eyes and knew there was more going on within him than he could convey. Denise intensified her research into how to help her son. She and her husband learned about the need for children with autism to work directly with trained therapists in an intensive program. Matthew was in some form of therapy for at least forty hours each week. Denise engaged and trained six to eight therapists to work with Matthew, using applied behavioral analysis and an artful integration of occupational and speech therapies, art, and other modalities. "I ran Matt's program like a business," Denise remarks, "We collected data and took copious notes to assess his progress. We shared the results with all the other therapists and hosted weekly team meetings in an effort to consistently implement the therapies and help Matt succeed."

Denise had a vision for her son. While she had no idea what he was capable of in those days, she wanted to help him fulfill his potential to the greatest degree possible. And perhaps, while unaware of it, Denise was developing her own life purpose at the same time. Both of these motivations put Denise into everyday action.

"I did that for about four years, including serving as Matt's chief therapist and interventionist. I also wound up in the hospital with exhaustion," Denise recalls, sadly. "When I began feeling stronger, I connected with other mothers, and there was one in particular who shared the same vision." In time, together with developmental pediatrician Dr. Raun Melmed and Cindy Schneider, a mother and doctor, Denise followed in her own mother's footsteps, her goal not only to help her own family, but also to provide the same vision of a healthy and whole life for other families confronting autism. Denise, Dr. Melmed, and Dr. Schneider cofounded SARRC. Denise's purpose was now solidified. For the first time, she had people with whom to share her burden and questions, and she had a supportive base to help make her vision a reality.

Denise flashes back to a pivotal moment: Matthew was five and still was not speaking. He'd been working with therapists for three years, but because she still could not communicate with her son, Denise wondered if any of their work was sinking in. She had a lesson that involved a trip to the park. "I took chalk with me and drew all kinds of shapes on the concrete: squares, circles, octagons, rectangles, and triangles. When I was finished, Matthew placed his hand over mine and began spelling the name of each shape underneath its picture with perfection!" This was a true milestone for Denise and Matthew. She understood that he was able to learn and that he had already amassed a great deal of knowledge. Matthew discovered a medium through which he could communicate with his mother. It was an enormous breakthrough for both of them.

That discovery has blossomed over the years. "Matthew is our human GPS system and calculator, able to solve triple-digit multiplication problems in his head," Denise says proudly. "He's a very visual learner and has an excellent memory. Recalling information correctly and then applying it functionally, however, continues to be a great challenge for him."

In spite of his age and the skills he has developed, Matthew is still vulnerable. Denise explains, "Because he now has an adult appearance, people have adult expectations of him that he just doesn't fulfill." In spite of his vulnerability, Matthew's excellent progress is due in large part to Denise's commitment.

The cofounders of SARRC initially ran the organization from their homes and offices. Then in 1998, they moved into their first facility, which totaled 1,800 square feet. Within a few months, they expanded the space to 4,000 square feet. SARRC continued to branch out into new programming, in essence growing up with the kids they served. Today SARRC's footprint consists of an 18,000-square-foot Campus for Exceptional Children and a separate 10,000-square-foot Vocational & Life Skills Academy. SARRC also has a presence throughout the region in clinical sites, schools, community venues, nonprofits, businesses, and more.

Denise began with a purpose that propelled her: helping Matthew. She then coupled it with a second purpose, which involved helping other children and families in similar situations. This led to two visions: one for her son and one for SARRC. With these as her guiding forces, Denise directed her actions diligently, tirelessly, and with incredible results.

Denise explains, "The autism spectrum represents many disorders, which adds to the complexity of our research. There is still so much we don't know about autism and so much we must learn in order to provide the most effective interventions to our kids. SARRC is a place where parents can turn for help and for hope. We have developed programs to fortify families with good information so they can be the best decision-makers possible for their children and their families.

"Since our founding, we have ardently promoted early intervention, and that continues today. Part of our mission is to educate doctors, teachers, therapists, and families to look for the early signs and symptoms of autism. The sooner a child is diagnosed, the sooner interventions can take place."

When Denise speaks about Matthew and the programs and visions of SARRC, she weaves the pieces in and out of one another. Matthew's needs served as an impetus for developing SARRC's programs and, in turn, those programs have helped Matthew effectively address his next developmental stage. "SARRC has been growing up for fourteen years," Denise states, "with a new and larger generation of kids affected by autism. As they've changed and developed, SARRC has grown and changed too."

As Matthew and hundreds of thousands of children with autism have reached that precipice of adulthood, SARRC is aggressively advancing vocational training, employment, and residential development programs. "The vision that was once driven by wanting Matthew to learn and communicate has expanded to encompass much more. It focuses on the active, productive lives men and women with autism can have in their communities and in society. This is crucial, particularly when you consider the aging populations whose parents are also aging. We wonder who will care for our sons and daughters when we're no longer able to do so," Denise explains.

Denise's ultimate vision is to build a future for individuals with autism that provides them with opportunities for friends, jobs, a home, and communities that support them. "Of course," Denise adds, "my ultimate vision is to discover the cause of autism, how we can stop it, and the most effective therapeutic interventions that respond to the different types of autism."

In the quiet of the night, when Denise is lying awake, her vision expands yet again. She thinks that there is so much more to do. "We are not there yet," she says. "I feel very good about the thousands of families that SARRC assists each year. The kids we see at SARRC are as important to their parents as Matthew is to me. Together, we're stronger, we'll find more answers, and we have even greater hope about the future. That's what inspires me. And even when I'm tired, it energizes and motivates me to do more."

Find more information about SARRC at www.autismcenter.org.

Purpose and Vision

One of the habits in Stephen Covey's *The 7 Habits of Highly Effective People* is, "Begin with the end in mind." Knowing what you want to achieve is the first step in setting your direction. Sometimes, however, we must first explore a number of paths to see what is right for us. It is also possible to walk our path awhile before we realize precisely what our destination is. Sometimes we'll travel a path for a time, and it will lead us to another path that may be even better aligned with our search for meaning. While your LifePath may resemble planning a trip in which you know your destination, it is also possible – perhaps even more likely – that finding your direction in life will involve a process of experimentation and exploration.

The ultimate end you wish to achieve – what will in essence become your legacy – is your vision. Vision takes the concept of purpose to a new level, including the world you wish to create over the long term. A vision is aspirational and inextricably linked to your purpose. It's where your role as a heartisan comes into play. You may be inspired initially with a vision that becomes the springboard for defining your purpose. Or, you may first uncover your purpose, which then leads to creating a vision. It does not matter which comes first. It is essential to understand why both are important, that they work in tandem, and that together they define your direction and the personal legacy you wish to create.

Denise Resnik's journey illustrates this point. Initially, her only goal was to support her son and find solutions for him. Matthew's autism was the impetus for her purpose. Soon, however, this vision expanded to helping other children and their parents. At some point, her pursuit became a path and she developed a vision for both Matthew and for SARRC. Denise's purpose and vision continued to grow and evolve as she learned more and as Matthew grew. We will discuss the synergy of vision and purpose in greater detail in the coming pages.

Vision

Your vision depicts what you aspire to create and describes what success looks like. It illustrates your ideal view of the world and certain benefits or results that will be realized. Your vision focuses on your intended outcome. Good visions capture and spark others' imagination, are easy to recall, and paint a brilliant mental picture of the future.

A vision statement describes your aspiration in words. It may also serve as an ongoing source of inspiration and motivation, a continual reminder of your goal. You may use it to inspire and motivate others to join your work or your cause.

Reverend Martin Luther King's dream was that the United States would, as a nation, "rise up and live out the true meaning of its creed: 'We hold these truths to be self-evident: that all men are created equal.'" His statement that "children will one day live in a nation where they will not be judged by the color of their skin but by the content of their character," represents a huge societal vision. His vision inspired millions of people and reflected his purpose in life. He created a compelling image that added momentum and direction to the Civil Rights Movement and is an aspiration that lives on today, even long after his tragic death.

The word vision can imply something grandiose, and your vision may be just that. A vision can also be quite personal and intimate. It is important to reiterate that you need not be pursuing a gigantic agenda to live a meaningful, fulfilling life. Your LifePath can be as big or as close-to-home as you like. We recommend beginning with a modest vision and then growing it as you feel comfortable and motivated to do so.

A vision should answer the questions:

- What am I aspiring to achieve?
- What does success look like?
- What is the future I am trying to create?

A vision should define success. Make yours as aspirational and inspirational as possible, creating mental images – a vivid picture – to inspire, create, clarify, engage others, and impel them to action. Then live your vision by emulating it through your actions.

"Vision without action is merely a dream. Action without vision is simply passing the time. Action with vision can change the world."
— Joel Barker

By adding Vision to our "Cycle of Inspiration and Personal Fulfillment" we illustrate its central role and guiding influence. Vision is shown in the center, since your vision may change as other parts in the model evolve. It works in tandem with your values as a light that guides you to create a life of meaning and purpose. The Cycle is now complete.

CYCLE OF INSPIRATION AND PERSONAL FULFILLMENT

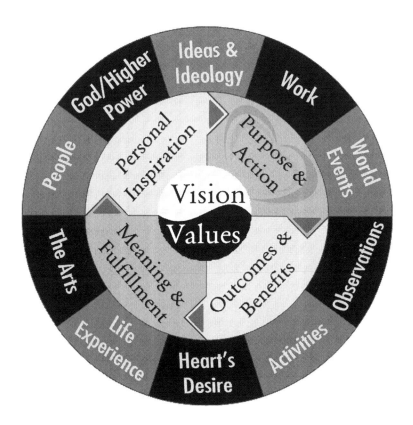

Purpose

For our discussions, purpose refers to the reason for doing something or for why something exists. It is easy to see Denise Resnik's purpose. She founded SARRC to help develop a fulfilling and contributing life for her son, to promote acceptance and inclusion of people with autism within the community, to help other families who are dealing with this series of disorders, and ultimately, to work toward a cure. Denise's purpose began from a very personal motivation and grew into something much larger.

Your own purpose may be very similar or quite different. Your purpose is, in part, self-determined, arising from your various interests and activities. You probably already have several purposes, based on the different roles in your life – being a member of a family, organization, department, community, school, or team. Beyond these, you may have chosen to pursue a greater purpose or calling in which you can have a significant impact on others or make a difference in the world. This may be local and intimate, global in nature, or anywhere in between. The scope is less important than having a purpose that is meaningful and personal for you.

The word purpose can also refer to an outcome you intend to achieve. To make the distinction between this definition of purpose and a "reason for doing something," as discussed above, we will refer to the former as a purpose-related vision.

A statement of purpose answers questions such as:

- What do I stand for?
- What is my cause or calling?
- How do I want to leave my mark on the world?
- What breakthroughs am I striving to create?
- What contribution do I want to be known for when people speak of me?

Why have a purpose? Why try to make a difference? Why try to give back or pay it forward? Why work to delight others through your art, or athleticism or ingenuity? A significant aspect of our humanity includes the desire to improve the world and help others who may be less fortunate. Many religions teach that we can't be whole while part of the world is broken. We can't live without suffering when others are suffering. Part of becoming whole ourselves comes from helping others find wholeness. This is how we all move forward. A purpose gives us a means of creating a greater good. And in the process, we make our own life a blessing by doing so with a willing heart.

You can take the initiative to get involved by serving meals to the homeless in a soup kitchen, visiting someone who is elderly and alone, walking for a medical cure, signing on with your community theatre group, developing a product that enhances everyday living, or myriad other ways. The reason for doing so will become clear when you experience the great feeling that comes with contributing to a cause or helping someone in need.

This will likely further motivate you to work toward your purpose.

How you ultimately pursue your purpose affects others who benefit from your actions – those who benefit directly, as well as those

> Your sense of personal fulfillment in life evolves from what you actually do – your actions and the accomplishments or progress they generate.

who see you as a role model and are inspired by your example. Ultimately, pursuit of your purpose will generate meaning and fulfillment for you.

Action

As we've mentioned, purpose without action is empty; it's simply a noble idea. Combining action with purpose is the key to experiencing fulfillment. The marriage of these two concepts generates the progress and produces the results that enable you to realize your vision and find ultimate satisfaction in life.

Your sense of personal fulfillment in life evolves from your actions and the progress they generate. Your personal feelings of self worth and your value in the eyes of others stem less from your beliefs and knowledge of what you can do, and more from the actions you take and the impact they make.

Major breakthroughs in most arenas are often incremental – and may result from the work of many – whether in cultural change, health care, justice, civil rights, politics, economic development, freedom, education, business, or other areas. Small successes build on one another, eventually leading to a tipping point. Nonetheless, these smaller breakthroughs are equally essential to the big ones, the big ones frequently accomplished by people who stood on the shoulders of those who laid the groundwork. Remember this as you begin to take action toward your purpose. It will help keep you motivated and prevent you from giving up if you do not see results as quickly as you had imagined.

Dr. Martin Luther King's dream, as we know, was not fulfilled in his tragically short life. Others built on his legacy and have continued his work. Some were people who worked with him. Many others, however, were inspired by his example and took up the cause in the years that followed. All these individuals helped drive the movement forward. Every breakthrough, whether large or small, has been significant. And, of course, Dr. King's work and journey continue to this day.

Similarly, Denise Resnik does not expect that a cure for autism spectrum disorders will be found in her lifetime. Yet she is committed to generating funds and supporting research toward this end. In the meantime, each discovery and every new understanding gleaned from SARRC's research creates a richer life for Matthew and others like him. Every action in Denise's and SARRC's parallel journeys moves her closer to realizing her vision.

It is hard to make and sustain big changes all at once. Sometimes you need to shift your direction in small degrees, analogous to the degrees on a compass, as discussed in Zuhdi Jasser's story. By adjusting your path incrementally, you will gradually reach the new path and direction you desire. Your new path and direction will take you to new places, enabling you to create a future that is different from your present. These small degrees of change and incremental breakthroughs will accumulate and facilitate long-term success.

Fulfillment evolves from every breakthrough, no matter the size or scope. It may increase as you see the mounting impact of your own efforts as well as those who may be working side-by-side with you.

Answers to the following questions can help you define your life purpose. They may require significant thought and soul searching, and may take time to uncover. Sometimes thoughts and ideas need to percolate before crystallizing.

What do I care about and wish to address?

Both parts of this question are crucial. You must have deep feelings or passion about your purpose and be willing to make a commitment to pursuing it. This requires time and effort. If one element or the other is missing, your journey toward developing a meaningful, fulfilling life will likely fall short of your expectations. The two, together, form the engine for your journey.

How will I create value?

The methods you choose for pursuing your purpose represent your unique way of creating value. Choosing activities that align with your interests and talents is important for your success and personal joy. Play to your strengths and build on them. Part of this equation is deciding where and with whom you want to work. Think about logical starting points and what would be comfortable for you as a first step or subsequent step. Relationships are essential to personal fulfillment, so consider partnering with people and organizations that share your values and passions.

How will I create meaning and fulfillment for myself?

In order to be most meaningful, your work must benefit both others and yourself. Just like a performer is reinforced by the applause of his/her audience, almost all of us need some form of tangible or intangible return for our efforts. The centerpiece of that return is the fulfillment you experience as a result of your work. This is not about being selfish. It's about replenishing the energy and aspirations that propel your journey.

PATHFINDER MODEL

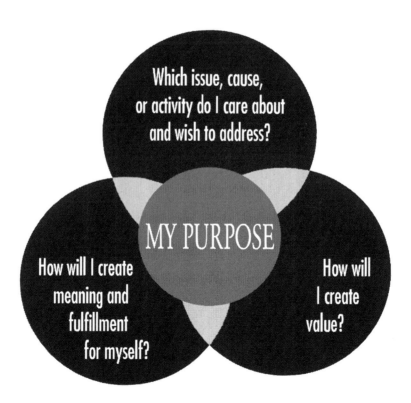

Establishing Your Direction and Purpose: Heartisan Pathfinder Card-Sort Exercise

The next step in the process involves exploring questions that will help you assess or refine your purpose. These questions are quite broad, and intended as thought starters. To help you explore them in greater depth and identify possible paths to pursue, we have developed a web-based exercise for considering alternatives. It's a fun, easy way to identify options, starting points, and/or next steps. This simple exercise will assist you in organizing your interests and desires. You can do this activity alone, or with your spouse, family, friends, classmates, or others to help you to define your path and the possibilities you would like to explore.

INNER QUEST
To what/whom am I committed?
What do I need right now?

OUTER QUEST
How can I balance my commitment to others with my own needs?

Visit FindFulfillFlourish.com and click on Find Your Purpose: Heartisan Pathfinder Exercise. Use Coupon Code GBC3MN24 for a complimentary three-month premium membership and access to the Heartisan Pathfinder exercise.

Complete the card sort exercise. We highly recommend that you put the book down now and take the time to complete this exercise. It will give you a much better idea of your values and how they interact with your purpose and LifePath. Spending these fifteen to thirty minutes – that's all it takes – will give you greater insight into your interests, curiosities, and strengths.

Food for Thought as You Initiate Your Pathfinder Card Sort

Sometimes a person chooses very few cards. If this is you, congratulations! Your interests and desires are very clear. Other individuals will find themselves sitting with a stack of cards in every pile. This is great too, because it reflects many interests or arenas from which to initiate growth and change. Nevertheless, you may feel overwhelmed if you find yourself with many cards, especially if you are engaging in this process for the first time. We suggest you narrow your options to your top two choices in each category in order to make your choices more manageable. Regardless of the results of your card sort, keep in mind that the purpose is to identify priorities and possibilities to pursue. The directions will be more thoroughly explained online, before you begin the exercise.

NAVIGATIONAL POINTS

- Use the Heartisan Pathfinder Cards to address the three "My Purpose" questions.
- Your purpose is unique to you, and reflects your values, ideals, and your heart.
- Use the Purpose Pathfinder Cards to identify and define your purpose.
- Your purpose and vision should be linked.
- Draft a personal vision describing the future you wish to create that aligns with your values.
- Identify specific actions you can take as the next steps in your journey.
- Engage others in your purpose and vision.

VISUALIZATION EXERCISES

Virtually nothing will help you manifest your goals faster than taking deliberate time to see them already complete. Here are two exercises you can use to begin visualizing your dream, goal, or LifePath.

Active Visualization

In your mind, form a picture, or a series of pictures, of your intended creation. See what it looks like, feels like, smells like, sounds like, and even tastes like, if that applies. Next, picture yourself experiencing this creation as if it were real. If your vision is job-related, picture your workspace with you in it. What are your daily tasks and routines? Picture yourself doing them. If you want to become a public speaker, picture yourself standing in front of a large crowd. Envision the emcee introducing you. Experience what it would feel like to have the audience welcome you with warm applause.

As you begin to visualize your creation, eliminate any doubts about your ability to have/create/experience your goal. Stem the negative self-talk and silence the censor in your head that tells you all the reasons it's just not possible. Replace those thoughts with the image of your creation, and counter any negatives with positive affirmations. Remember, you manifest what you concentrate on.

The most important aspect of this visualization process is that you see it as though you are doing it – not as if you are watching yourself do it. Although you most certainly are directing this vision, your perspective is as the actor in your movie, not the director.

Create a Vivid Visual

Craft a concrete picture of your creation. This can be an actual snapshot or photograph of the thing, if it's something tangible, like a trip to Ireland. It can be a collage of words and pictures related to your goal; it can be a treasure map or a timeline; it can be a cartoon panel.

It doesn't matter what the vivid visual is, as long as it is a pictorial representation of your goal. Once you've created the vivid visual, put it in a place where you can easily see it so that it will be a constant reminder of your goal.

Know that once you begin this visualization process of manifesting your goal, nothing can stop you from achieving it.

For additional exercises on identifying a purpose and developing a vision, visit FindFulfillFlourish.com:

- *Click the Find Your Purpose tab and use the electronic "Heartisan Pathfinder Exercise."*
- *Click on the Book & Tools tab for additional worksheets and activities.*

Chapter 6

Spirituality: If You Breathe, You're Spiritual

Breathing life

Feeling your purpose inside of you

Expressing your purpose outwardly

Welcoming Spirituality: Carolyn Manning and the Welcome to America Project

Carolyn Manning's life changed forever on September 11, 2001, as she learned that her brother-in-law, Terence, who had been attending a breakfast at the World Trade Center, was killed in the terrorist attack. Understandably, her first response was shock. Having grown up Catholic, Carolyn had been taught by her parents to turn the other cheek and always look for the best in people, but she had no way to make any sense of this. "When I was a child, my mom would tell me the simplest way to avoid bad dreams was to pray to God for protection, and that God would respond. A simple prayer and no more bad dreams. Now, I had to find a way to fit into my world the murder of an innocent person I knew, and of so many, many other innocent people," Carolyn reflected.

"Why would somebody do that? And how was I to reconcile this act with a favorite song I had memorized as a child, called The Prayer of St. Francis? It starts out, 'Lord, make me an instrument of your peace; where there is hatred, let me sow love.'" Carolyn felt compelled to find an answer to this question.

In the weeks and months that followed, she absorbed as much information as possible to help her understand why 9/11 had occurred. She immersed herself in the media to learn all the details and who the players were. She read newspapers, watched TV, and scoured web reports. She recalled seeing images that astounded and haunted her: strained addresses by President Bush, people who appeared to be Muslims burning American flags, the words *Allah al akbar* (praise be to Allah) repeated in photo after photo, and Muslims rejoicing at the destruction of the towers and the precious life within them.

Carolyn recalls thinking, "*These people who killed Terence were only a small group, and they do not represent a nation or a religion.* As I realized they were the minority, I thought, *We can't persecute a whole people for the actions of nineteen individuals.*"

Carolyn reflects back to one of her early experiences with religious differences. "When I was in first grade, I told my best friend, Lynn Mecus, a Lutheran, that my faith of Catholicism was the one true religion. She was incensed and demanded, 'How do you know that?'

"I responded with conviction and confidence, 'I learned it in church.'

"Lynn got right up and left my house. The next day, when I went to her house, she refused to play. Day after day, as this continued, I thought more and more about my words. Why would God give me His attention and deny another very good person because they had a different religion? I loved my faith, but maybe she loved her faith, too. Maybe God loved all the ways people worshiped Him.

"With this revelation, I went to the bathroom cabinet and pulled out a bobby pin and a blue bow. I did my best to make a hair ribbon and I again set off again for Lynn's house. This time she came to the door. I quickly stuck out my arm with the ribbon in my palm and said, 'Here, this is for you. I don't think my religion is the best anymore,' and left. The next day, Lynn came to my door with a store-bought red ribbon, and we once again began to play. We never discussed religion again. I think God liked seeing us play together. After all, we were both His creations. Now this lesson floated into my brain, all those decades later."

With that thought and memory in mind, Carolyn began to consider Islam. She recalls, "I hadn't given any thought to the Muslim faith prior to 2001. It seemed very different from Christianity, even from Judaism. I started to wonder more about Islam and I worried about those people who were not terrorists, those who were trying to live simple lives as Muslims."

On October 6, 2001, less than one month after Terence was killed, Carolyn saw a photo in the local newspaper of an Afghan Islamic family. The woman in the photo was wearing a hijab (head scarf). "I read the story and realized that her family was similar to my family. She had four kids, whereas I had five. Her father was murdered by the Taliban, after being forcibly removed from his home at gunpoint in the middle of the night. Their business and possessions were taken, and they fled Afghanistan. I realized that Al Queda wasn't just hurting Americans, that it was more general than that."

Carolyn says, "I believe God creates people as intrinsically good, yet God allows them free will. Al Queda and the Taliban, with their desire for power and thinking that they have the right to destroy life, are making very devastating choices. They are choosing evil. This is not God being evil; this is the free will of people being applied in an awful way."

Carolyn was still thinking about Al Queda and the Taliban as she read the article about the Afghan woman. The newspaper referred to her and her family as refugees. Carolyn looked at the word and thought, "What does that mean?"

She researched and explored what it meant to be a refugee, which affirmed her belief in the goodness of people, particularly those in the U.S. government. It had never occurred to her before that people were fleeing to the United States to live, much less that some were coming from the same country that was harboring Al Queda.

Carolyn was moved to wonder, *What kind of country are we?*

She further explains her thoughts at the time: "We, the Americans, can separate individuals and their actions from their country of origin. We can separate their actions from their religion, their race, or even the behavior of so many of their countrymen, judging them solely as individuals. I noticed how great a country we are, and my thoughts began to spiral. The same terrorism that is affecting our country is affecting innocent people in Afghanistan, and we were willing to offer these victims refuge. People from the same country as those who killed Terence were now sitting in a living room in Phoenix. As Americans, we seek to bring justice to those trying to destroy us, while simultaneously offering refuge in our country to their neighbors.

"I had two responses to this discovery. The first was that I was very proud that our country is so discerning and has a policy that accepts the world's homeless, even if only a small percent. Sure, there's much more we can do, but it made me feel good to be an American. My second thought was, 'We lost Terence, but at least I'm still in my country. The family in that article had to leave their country;

how must they feel right now? And how must it feel being an Afghan after 9/11? These innocent people became a target just because of what happened in their country.'" Carolyn's well of compassion is huge, and her sadness was palpable when she said, "I felt very sorry for them."

The article got Carolyn to thinking about what she could do, as one individual. "In honor of Terence, I wanted to reach out to this family in a way I saw as representative of all Americans. I wanted to welcome them to our country. I wanted to say to them, 'I have lost family to the hands of Al Queda, and you have lost family to the hands of the Taliban. We are both here in Phoenix and we have that in common.'"

It is clear in listening to Carolyn that in her paradigm, this is the most natural conclusion in the world. Others might not have had such a charitable response. Some might have decided to plot against anyone even resembling those who murdered their loved ones in the 9/11 attacks. Others might have become consumed by their own loss. But Carolyn made a connection between her own loss and grief and the loss and grief of others, whom some might have termed "enemy." She used this as an opportunity to reach out and help, to give a struggling refugee family a sense of belonging.

She followed up with the agency that had brought in the refugees, the International Rescue Committee. "I spoke with someone who didn't doubt me or question me when I told them I'd lost someone in 9/11 and I wanted to reach out to this refugee family. She was quite open, giving me the family's contact information. I then asked friends if they'd like to help this family make their house into a home.

"While I was seeking donations, I went to the refugees' apartment and met the family. They greeted me with a blank response when I told them why I had sought them out." Carolyn was initially disappointed by their response, but she quickly learned that refugees are very reluctant to trust strangers – any strangers. Refugees hesitate to share their stories or show their emotions because they don't know who truly has their best interests at heart. Cultural and religious norms may also discourage openness.

"I wanted to help anyway," Carolyn said. "I made flyers and put them out at the preschool. We took them to the grade school and to our church. I asked people to donate furniture and household items for a family that was a victim of terror. We soon had six pickup trucks and vans filled with donations. A local Girl Scout troop was among the volunteers who came to help us unload.

"Unexpectedly, there I was making this delivery, and the first thing I saw was all these other refugees. They all live together in designated apartment buildings when they arrive."

Phil, Carolyn's husband, steps in to add, "We brought so much stuff – way too much! We could've supplied two or three families with what we brought."

"Really," Carolyn responds, "we could have supplied five or six families, when we think of what we donate now." When asked why they brought so much, she answered, "Because that's what people donated. We had three cribs, so we brought them.

"When we arrived, lots of people were milling around. It seemed that our chosen family had met other Afghan families and had already created a community among themselves. All the men helped us unload. We picked one room and filled it with furniture. It was literally stacked from floor to ceiling. We realized we had way too much for a single family, but now we knew that the goods we brought would be divided among all the families. We could already see that each family would select items based on their needs. In addition to furniture, we brought toys, food, household supplies from Costco, wall hangings, you name it.

"This time, while I finally understood that I might never be real friends with this woman, the family was truly grateful, as were the other families. Their one discomfort was that they were sorry they had nothing to give to us in exchange for the gifts, because all of their things had been left behind or confiscated. They couldn't possibly have known that being able to give to them in their hardship was the biggest gift of all."

Carolyn says in retrospect, "Refugees undergo such an ordeal." She had initially hoped to become close to this Afghan mother with whom she had so much in common. But Carolyn's faith enabled her to move beyond her own desires of the moment, and in time, she came to understand the world through a refugee's eyes.

Carolyn observed that refugees generally seem to deal with their pain in two ways. The first are those who keep their past with them and wall it off as if it were a cyst. "It's part of your body, but separate, and it never goes away." These individuals allow their prejudices and hatred to thrive for the people who harmed them in their parent country. As America gives refuge to all, families from opposing forces might find themselves living in the same apartment building, and they could still be living out this hatred.

Others, she says, "try to release the past and allow little openings of their psyche, so you can see who they really are. When they let you in, some of their pain leaks out, and over time they heal." The good news is that most of the refugees she met are in the latter category.

After Carolyn's delivery, people continued to bring donations by her house, and Carolyn felt obliged to accept them. Her garage became her storage shed and was full to overflowing. "I called the International Rescue Committee and asked if they could arrange a pick-up. But still more donations came, and I knew I had to figure out how to give people receipts so they could claim their tax deductions. I kept telling God that if He wanted me to do this, He'd have to tell me how, because I didn't know how to do it."

On November 25, 2001, just ten short weeks after Terence was murdered in the World Trade Center attacks, Carolyn incorporated her endeavor as a nonprofit business, now called the Welcome to America Project (WTAP). "I went to the IRS website and downloaded the info to set it up. I called them again and again for help as I filled out the paperwork."

Then Bobbie called from Lock It Lockers, asking Carolyn if she could help by providing a free storage unit for the first year. "That was a sign from God that I was going to get some help." Carolyn then heard from Megan, a mom she knew from the preschool, who said, "I have time on my hands. I've seen you in your yard with furniture, and I'd like to help." The two women drove around with their babies, picking up and delivering furniture.

The business continued to grow this way. Each time Carolyn identified a need, she said, "God will provide someone to fill it." When she saw that she needed financial guidance and the ability to make donations tax deductible, she realized she had to find an accountant. "I always tried to find someone who would donate their services." She found her accountant, who is still with her, and later her Web designer.

"People weave in and out of WTAP; it's a community experience for them. They come and go when it suits them. The greatest thing people say to me is, 'I'm here when you need me.'" Carolyn learned that helping the refugees was not only filling the refugees' needs for home and rootedness, but it was filling a need for the people who volunteered, giving them a way to feel that they had used their time and energy in a worthy manner.

The number of volunteers grew, as did the continuous inpouring of refugees. Groups of people now approached Carolyn, offering to help. Interestingly, nearly all of the groups had religious affiliations. "There was a Jewish high school, the American Muslim Women's Association, a bar mitzvah project, Hindu helpers, and Bobbie was a practicing Buddhist." Today, thirty to forty individuals help regularly, while hundreds show up only once. WTAP currently delivers goods each week to three families, a process that requires the efforts of fifteen volunteers.

How do people find WTAP? "Mostly by word of mouth," Carolyn says, "through their school, or by someone who referred them. People Google 'refugees in Arizona' and they find us. We have been approached by interns, neighbors of neighbors ... everyone has their own path to our door."

> "I don't like asking people for things. I never did. Yet I was pushed to do the very thing that made me uncomfortable. That is how God works in our lives."

Carolyn reflects again on her spirituality. She says, "I don't like asking people for things. I never did. Yet I was pushed to do the very thing that made me uncomfortable. This is how God works in our lives. God pushes us past our own discomfort. I asked a guy I knew from church, but only as an acquaintance, to get up early and help me pick up a couch at six in the morning. That was God using me as an instrument."

Carolyn recalls what brought her to this guidepost. "I learned this lesson years ago from my teacher, Sister Donna Behensee, at my all-girls' Catholic high school. I don't think I ever told her, but I have thought of her so many times through the years. She taught me the Old and New Testaments the year after she returned from Calcutta, where she worked alongside Mother Teresa and the sisters from the Missionaries of Charity.

"What amazing stories Sr. Donna told us! I found the stories both enviable and terrifying. Being near Mother Theresa must have been so wonderful, but it was hard to imagine being brave enough to hold a dying, disheveled person in your arms. How could she agree to live in such filth and squalor? I knew then that I was not brave enough, and I felt ashamed. I felt cowardly knowing that my life was so good. I also knew that God had put enough resources on this earth so that no one had to go hungry or live on the street. But it just seemed too hard to be part of the solution to this problem. I knew I had a lot to give; I just didn't know how to give it."

Giving refugees, who come to the United States with little more than the clothes on their backs, the ability to turn their houses into homes is one way Carolyn is now part of the solution. It may not always be comfortable and it sometimes entails skills Carolyn does not feel she has mastered, but she believes she is called to engage in these challenges as part of fulfilling the spiritual work God has demanded of her.

WTAP continues to grow, and as it does, Carolyn gains deeper insight into the plight of the refugees. "We have served more than one thousand refugee families from thirty-one countries," Carolyn explains. "They are here escaping war, religious and ethnic persecution, rape, and torture. They have lost relatives they never had the chance to bury or grieve. Many have family members who are still trapped in their old country, and they work tirelessly to move them to the safety of the United States."

Carolyn and Robin met because Carolyn wanted to design a memorial service for the refugees, a place where they could say their goodbyes, plant seeds of renewal, and begin their lives in the U.S. with freshness and hope. Carolyn and Robin worked for the better part of a year with eleven clergy members of multiple faiths to form an interfaith service in which every refugee could take part. In an auditorium filled with hundreds of people, new immigrants, many of them wearing the traditional clothing of their cultures and homelands and escorting children and elderly, had the chance to mourn and start again.

Whether Carolyn realizes it or not, she has finally created the kind of relationships with these families she had been seeking when she organized her first donation. For these refugees to share their stories with her, the traumas they have lived through, the loved ones they still pray to bring to the United States, and their grief for all they have lost requires enormous trust. They feel safe with Carolyn. She has given such a gift to the refugees, not only with her furniture and toys, but through her caring heart and listening ear. Her commitment to these families did not end with providing them the material goods that would help them settle here. For Carolyn, part of sharing God's abundance and goodness involved enabling these new Americans to live lives of freedom and choice, which is exactly what she offered them through the memorial service.

"They needed a chance to say goodbye – because most of their loved ones never had burials or funerals. Some of their loved ones are still missing, and the refugees don't even know if they are alive. Saying goodbye creates an opening for them to breathe in forgiveness and gratitude for their lives and freedom, as well as allowing them to plant seeds for their future. We gave each person at the service a package of seeds to plant as a metaphor for growing their new lives here."

The memorial service also helped Carolyn turn a corner in her own life, for as a result of it, she decided to accept a management job in the office of the Arizona State Refugee Coordinator, and she now serves on the board of WTAP. She felt it was time to put the organization in the hands of others, and she is now in a position to truly affect policy change and help refugees' lives more substantially.

Carolyn reflects on the whole process of her work with refugees and God's place in her life. She says, "God was the push for this project from the beginning, from the very first step when we lost Terence." She adds, "Ever since I was a little girl, I wondered what God's will was for me. God's will is my daily prayer. I pray these words:

> Please tell me where You want me to go,
> And please tell me what You want me to do,
> And help me to be brave enough to do it.

"I even remember praying this in the first grade," Carolyn recounts, "and feeling the fear that was right behind it."

When Robin and Carolyn get together, they speak of God and spirituality. Though they are from different faiths, they find that they speak the same language. Fear motivates Carolyn to pray even harder. She recalls the fear when she saw all that furniture in her yard, and she prayed. "The fear is that the path is unknown, and it isn't smooth." But with faith, she can breathe. The fear diminishes, and Carolyn hears God telling her where to go and what to do again and again in her work with refugees. And while she may speak of her fear, it is clear from Carolyn's works that she is indeed very brave.

Breathing in her own spirituality in spite of doubts and fears, Carolyn has discovered her own purpose and LifePath. And through her actions, her spirituality grows continually stronger and becomes ever more meaningful.

For more information about the Welcome to America project, visit WTAP.org.

Spirituality and Life

A fascinating fact about the word spirituality is that it comes from the Latin word *spiritualis*, which is about breathing. Whether or not you believe in God, whether you are an atheist, one who needs scientific proof to acknowledge God's existence, or one who is a devout follower of a particular religion, if you are reading this, you are alive, which means you breathe. If you are alive and breathing, by definition you have spirit within you. How you choose to define that spirituality is unique to you. It is important for each of us to recognize, though, that spirit continually runs through you all of us. Some people define spirituality through

God, others through religion, and still others more loosely, relating more to the heart or the sacred.

Big deal. Why does any of this matter? Each one of us, regardless of our religious orientation, can understand the experience of awe. It can occur in the simplest and also in the oddest moments. It is common for new parents to experience awe when they see their first child born. Sometimes we feel it when we witness a sunset. Then there are those unexpected moments, like coming upon a tiny lizard and watching it do those funny little lizard pushups (this is the lizard breathing, by the way – he is having a moment of spirit), and marveling at how amazing it is that a creature only one-and-ah-half inches long can do pushups, even as he looks straight at you. Awe is that moment when you realize that life is a miracle, when you realize that something greater than you exists. And that something, whatever it is, is so big and so great that you can hardly fathom it. And yet, whatever that great big thing is, it goes on, because every day babies are born, the sun rises and sets, and lizards do breathing pushups.

As you witness and experience these moments, you realize that in some way, you too are a miracle. The fact that you breathe, see, listen, sit, walk, stand, and eat the pizza you've been pining for all day – the fact that your body works, grows, and changes – all of these things add up to the miracle that is you.

When we sit in this moment of awe, we are having an experience of spirit, of the sacred. Regardless of what you name it, the essence of the matter is that you are connecting, in that moment of awe, to that something that is greater than you. This awakening often inspires us to reach out to others, because we suddenly feel connected. It dawns on us that we are all part of a fabulous, interlacing web, connected by the Creator – whether you call that God or the Big Bang. Such awe and connection to the whole are what inspire many people to take on a task that is greater than themselves.

Reflecting this way may lead us to carefully consider our actions. Feeling part of the whole is what caused Carolyn Manning to ask, "How could someone just kill innocent people?" She was aware of the web that connects us all. It was this same understanding that enabled her to offer help and solace to a family she didn't know.

"There is no need for temples; no need for complicated philosophy. Our own brain, our own heart is our temple; the philosophy is kindness."
— Dalai Lama

As we see in Carolyn's story, the ripple effects of an act can be for good or for evil, generating more good or wreaking further evil in its wake. The 9/11 attacks were acts of horrendous evil. The fear and destruction that followed in their aftermath have been felt ever since, the insidious effects of that evil. Fabulously, though, some did not succumb to the evil. While evil certainly perpetuates more evil, it can also generate good by strengthening convictions for positive visions – many responded positively to this awful tragedy. Numerous individuals – both professional first responders and ordinary citizens – worked to help others escape the doomed buildings. Others showed up at the bombing sites to help the victims. And people like Carolyn, who experienced a loss she could not understand, took her first opportunity to reach out in kindness to other victims of tragedy.

A verse in the Jewish tradition, from Ethics of the Fathers says, *"Mitzvah goreret mitzvah."* It means that one good deed causes another good deed. Why is this? Because it makes you and others feel good. What's wonderful about this phrase is that it's unclear whether it means that if you do a good deed, it will cause you to do another, or if doing something nice for someone else will cause him or her to do something nice for you. Or for someone else. Or all of these. And so the wave continues in many directions, never-ending. Eventually, the ripple caused by your actions returns to you, as well.

That good feeling creates smiles and warmth. It causes you to breathe, enhancing your spirit and your life. The more you invest in good deeds and good projects, the more your life and the lives of those around you are enhanced. And when you lie down at the end of the day, you have that great tired feeling that comes from

Most of us have heard the term "higher purpose." What is the difference between an ordinary purpose and a higher one? Robin had a conversation about this with Ella, a high school student. Ella mentioned that she wanted her boyfriend to have a purpose.

Robin: "What kind of purpose?"

Ella: "Any purpose, as long as he has a purpose."

Robin: "What if his purpose is harmful?"

Ella: "Well, I mean a purpose that helps others and makes a difference in the world. A purpose that is good. And noble."

knowing you did something worthwhile, something that helped others in some way, and about which you can feel very proud. All because of a little spirit.

A compelling passage from the Talmud, a compendium of Jewish law, is also found, in subtle variation, in the Qur'an: "Whosoever saves a life, it's as if that person has saved a whole universe." – *Tractate Sanhedrin*

The magic in this quote is its message that each individual is an entire universe. Each of us, in our uniqueness, makes a contribution that no other person can make. It is important for us to remember this when we become concerned about doing something the right way. While we recommend some guidelines to provide lights on your roadway, remember that your path is unique to you, and whichever choice speaks to your heart is the right one for you.

President Barack Obama used this quote in his 2009 speech in Cairo, with a completely different intention. He was addressing the Arab world, encouraging citizens of these countries to make a greater investment in their cultures, to choose to save life rather than destroy it. His statement connects beautifully with Carolyn and her work with WTAP. How interesting it might be to think that one of the ripples of Carolyn's care and kindness was that it touched our president, who took a stand for good among all the Arab nations.

So right about now, you might find yourself thinking, "Oh my goodness. My lifeguarding skills are pretty weak. What would I ever do if I found myself in a position to save a life?" It might be simpler than you think.

Hannah cherishes the values of compassion, kindness, and service and demonstrates them with her gentle, sensitive manner. She recently learned that resi-

Robin: "Yes, I understand. That's what we mean by a higher purpose."

At the age of seventeen, Ella understood how important it was that the people with whom she maintained close relationships were also pursuing a higher purpose. She wanted to associate with people who had compatible spirits and embraced similar values. She recognized that without this characteristic, they would have little common ground, which would limit her interest to no more than a casual friendship.

dents of nearby nursing homes and assisted living facilities desired spiritual support and services. Each week, she schedules time to visit and conduct services in two or three places, bringing comfort, company, and inspiration to the residents.

Like Hannah, each time you feed a hungry person, every donation you make to an organization that helps others, every song you perform that brings a smile to the audience's face, each instance when you counsel someone in pain or grief, you are in some way saving a person's life. Generating light when it's lacking is a way of taking small steps to save a life.

But how is this saving an entire universe?

It all goes back to awe. Every human was created from the same template, but each of us unique. There is no one else in the world exactly like you. You are a one and only. And you hold an entire universe of individuality inside of you; no one else can or will contribute exactly what you contribute. Every step you take to preserve or enhance the life of another is enhancing that individual's ability to make their unique contribution.

Creating Light

President George H.W. Bush, both in his 1989 inaugural address and again in his 1991 State of the Union address, used the metaphor of "a thousand points of light" to capture this phenomenon. In his speech to the U.S. Congress he said, "We can find meaning and reward by serving some purpose higher than ourselves – a shining purpose, the illumination of a thousand points of light. It is expressed by all who know the irresistible force of a child's hand, of a friend who stands by you and stays there – a volunteer's generous gesture, an idea that is simply right."

These are the moments when spirituality is transformational and inspires us to live a more purpose-infused and meaningful life – when we become one of those thousand points of light, which hopefully grow into millions and millions. By living our spirituality, we in turn inspire others. The light we create makes a difference and illuminates our purpose.

Looking at Carolyn's story, we can see how her point of light affected so many others, both individuals and groups. Initially, it affected the lives of the family she learned about in the newspaper. Then her light touched the woman she spoke with at the International Rescue Committee. Shortly thereafter, her light impacted all the families she met the day she made that first delivery of too much furniture. There were the people she engaged to help her make that delivery. And from there, her light touched more families and hundreds of volunteers. Her single point of light reached out to touch more than a thousand others. Together they form a stunning constellation.

INNER QUEST
How would you describe your spirituality?

OUTER QUEST
How do you outwardly demonstrate it?

We may not always know, like Carolyn is fortunate to know, when something we have done changes someone's life. We never know when something we might have said or done that seemed insignificant at the time – perhaps something so seemingly trivial that we don't even remember it – may come back to us years later.

Robin knows a teacher who had a very difficult student. She often struggled with the decision of whether or not to expel him. The teacher tirelessly tried to work with him, but often felt her efforts were fruitless. Years later, she ran into her student, now a man in his thirties, at a convention. He thanked her for how kind she had been to him all those years ago. He told her that until her class, he'd felt that nobody believed in him and he had been considering suicide – but she changed that. The teacher was surprised by this news about how vulnerable he had been, because she remembered only her frustration with him. He told her that she had been instrumental in helping him to discover self-respect, that she inspired him to become a teacher, and that she was pivotal in helping him make his life successful. Now he is doing the same for his students.

This teacher's story is very tangible proof that our actions count – even though we may be unaware of the impact. We never truly know when we will be someone's inspiration. When we give the best we have to offer, our impact is often far greater than we realize or expect. If we move through our days with this intention, we can only bring good to the world around us.

Another example is R.D., who works in structural integration, a form of bodywork that helps people achieve greater freedom of movement. His office is in the arts district of Oak Park, Illinois. Several times each year, the district hosts arts festivals, and R.D. is one of the business owners who opens his office to local artists, allowing them to turn his office space into a gallery. He helps them hang their work and then opens the "studio" as a showplace during the weekend's extended festival hours.

R.D. continues to exhibit the pieces for the month following each opening. Then the artists retrieve the pieces that haven't sold, and several months later, the whole process begins again. R.D. participates in these art shows to support local artists while he beautifies his work-space. He is simultaneously meeting new people and contributing to ap-preciation of the visual arts in gener-al. The fact that R.D.'s impact may be more immediate and obvious to him than the teacher in the previous story does nothing to diminish its effect on the artists who benefit from his generosity.

> Your spirituality is manifested through your higher purpose. Spirituality is felt on the inside and expressed on the outside. It's the dynamic energy that enables you to make a positive difference.

Connection to Finding Meaning and Purpose

Your spirituality is manifested through your higher purpose. Spirituality is felt on the inside and expressed on the outside. It's the dynamic energy that en-ables you to make a positive difference. Some might say it is doing God's work on earth, while others believe it is a personal force that breathes life into causes greater than ourselves. Regardless, it's all a form of spirituality and a source of inspiration.

Judaism teaches that we are partners with God in creation, that God made the heavens and the earth and everything within them in six days. And on the seventh day, as Midrash (Jewish commentary) tells us, God rested. Now God asks us to be partners every day in continuing to make the world a better place.

Pastor Joel Osteen said it well on his television show, while preaching on the importance of investing. He made the distinction between the idea of investing in resources (creating a financial legacy to leave our children and their children) versus the concept of investing in people. While the former is a good thing – most of us want to ensure that our children have enough resources to take care of them-selves after we're gone – money doesn't provide our children with tools, skills, and values. The true investment in our children's future would be taking the time and energy necessary to teach them values, purpose, and meaning. Our legacy would then be one of ideas, beliefs, values, actions, and opportunity.

Every individual, Osteen said, has a set of skills and expertise – whether it be parenting, cooking, praying, educating, growing food, architecture, or designing computer programs. Let's pass on those skills, investing in the people we love and in our community. By doing so, we give of ourselves and plant seeds for the future. In this way, the beauty of our contributions lives on and enriches others, and simultaneously, we live on through them. Joel Osteen was describing, in spiritual terms, the essential characteristics of a heartisan.

Carolyn Manning exemplifies Joel Osteen's teaching. She and her husband have five children. Each of them has watched their parents' example. Not only do the kids help with the Welcome to America Project, but they grew up watching people leave couches and cribs on their lawn. Throughout their youth, they witnessed people come to their home with trucks in the early morning to help with deliveries. They saw their mom learning business skills and overcoming her own fears and obstacles so she could better serve people in need.

Additionally, Carolyn embeds these values in her children as a part of their daily responsibilities. She and her husband have set up a point system in their family. When their children perform good deeds, they receive points that allow them to participate in the activities of their choice. Some of the things that earn points are the basics we might expect: doing homework, keeping their rooms clean, and completing chores around the house; others are related to being of service, such as doing volunteer work or spending time with the church youth group. In so many ways, Carolyn is passing on her learning and life skills to her children.

Teaching her children and working with WTAP are not the end of the effect Carolyn has on the world. She knew she needed to expand her staff and replace herself in the business in order for the WTAP to grow and so that she could move to a position that allowed her to make a greater difference for future refugees. Carolyn taught and coached the staff at WTAP before she left, providing them with the skills and insights to effectively serve Phoenix's refugee population. As she stepped beyond herself, striving to reach her vision more fully, she simultaneously modeled for the WTAP staff and her children the values of perseverance, caring for others, and seeking justice. All of this is part of her active spirituality.

We always come full circle: spirituality is about breathing, and breathing is about life. Through our spirituality and actions, we can breathe renewal, awakening, and freshness – even healing – into the world around us. We can invigorate life for one or for millions. Whether we share a smile with the grocery cashier, bring food to the elderly, plant crops in poverty-stricken villages in Peru, or work toward a cause like Carolyn's, our spirit – our very breath – can affect the lives of others around the globe. All is possible, as long as we're willing to connect to that breath and drive it with purpose, vision, and continued action. You are a universe, indeed.

NAVIGATIONAL POINTS

- Spirituality is breath: it breathes life into who you are, how you design your life, and the positive difference you make.

- The essence of spirituality is that there is something greater than us.

- There's more than one path to spirituality. You do not have to believe in God or follow a religion to have a spiritual life.

- Your spirituality is manifested in your higher purpose. Your spirituality is felt internally and expressed externally.

- Spirituality produces greater meaning in our lives when we connect it with pursuit of a higher purpose.

- You are a universe, which means that you provide a unique contribution.

- Every act you do has a ripple effect. Your ripple can be for good.

- Your ripples will come back to you, whether immediately or in the long term.

- You are a point of light, and your light ignites the lights of others.

APPLYING THE CONCEPTS TO YOUR LIFE

1. How do I define my spirituality?
2. What brings my spirituality to life?
3. What inspires me ... gives me a sense of awe?
4. What enhances my spirit ... my sense of awe?
5. What am I connecting to that is greater than myself?
6. How do I demonstrate the good or inspiring energies that breathe out of me?
7. What kinds of seeds do I want to plant?
8. How can I integrate my spirituality more deeply into my purpose?

9. Who are the others with whom I share my spirituality?

10. Which places awaken or revive my spirituality?

11. What kinds of exercises, rituals, or practices help me connect to my spirit?

Chapter 7

Relationships: Why You Need Others and Others Need You

Connecting with others

Engaging and supporting partnerships

Building resources

A World of Relationships: Kelly Campbell and The Village Experience

Kelly Campbell walks through the small fishing village of Mbita, Kenya, on the shores of Lake Victoria. This isolated community, two to three hours from the closest city, is struggling. In their search for solutions to their long-standing economic challenges, Mbita's leaders have persuaded Kelly and The Village Experience group to visit their community. The community is very poor and chronically short of needed goods. It is quite costly for them to secure basic necessities due to the long drive over rough roads to the nearest communities.

Mbita's residents want to improve their economy and create jobs for themselves, and in turn, help their children attain a better education. The result will be higher living standards for the entire village. People in other parts of the country have heard of Kelly's work, and how she is helping impoverished communities move themselves from poverty and dependence to self-sufficiency and independence. They hope she can help them do the same. They know Kelly works to help these villagers realize their dreams.

When Kelly arrived in Mbita, she was warmly welcomed. The hospitality of the townspeople was exceptional, and she responded in kind. She focused her attention on developing relationships. Although this was not her first trip to the area, her primary objective is always to build trust. She listens and learns.

Kelly observed the desire and enthusiasm of the villagers, evaluating their needs and requests. Energized by the possibilities, she explained her role in helping the villagers to the group of international students traveling with her on The Village Experience tour. Kelly's vision is to enable the villagers to develop the ability to guide their own destiny.

In Mbita, Kelly helps the villagers renovate a store, including the acquisition and installation of a mosquito net. She guides them in getting other businesses off the ground, as she has done in other communities, often beginning with agricultural enterprises. The current project is a chicken coop, which will provide the families with chickens to eat and eggs to sell. In the future, new chicks will keep the business going and potentially help others start new businesses. Addressing the community's need for food is primary, and a project such as this immediately puts the villagers on a road to greater health and self-sufficiency.

The women of the village present business ideas for their crafts and artisan work. Kelly funded the purchase of three sewing machines that will enable the women to be more productive and create more items to sell.

Once the basics are in place, Kelly teaches the villagers how to run their businesses. These newly invigorated, well-run businesses begin to generate money, some of which pays the salaries of new teachers in the local school. Other income enhances community services; as a result, the entire village becomes more prosperous.

Deep joy is fostered by these businesses – the residents of Mbita now know they are emerging from the threat of hunger and poverty. This realization produces an air of possibilities. Soon the villagers generate more new ideas. They want to erect a party tent for weddings, funerals, and celebrations within the community. They see the potential the tent has to generate income through rentals to their own residents and those of nearby villages. The people of Mbita are proactively creating their own brighter future.

During a subsequent trip to Mbita, Kelly visits a school she helped the village renovate. It looks fabulous. With funding now in place for new teachers, the children receive a higher-quality education in a healthier environment. Mbita's future is being created before her eyes.

This story exemplifies the important work that Kelly and The Village Experience do in many impoverished communities in Africa, Central America, the Middle East, and Asia. In addition to the people she assists in Kenya, people in Uganda, South Africa, Thailand, Guatemala, India, Ethiopia and Jordan are touched by her work.

Kelly's sister, Anne, works to create a market for the goods produced by the villagers. The Village Experience store in Indianapolis is one such outlet. It's a fair trade store that sells art, clothing, and handicrafts brought back from the developing countries the volunteers visit. This is all part of Kelly's and Anne's vision to foster financial self-sufficiency and sustainability for people in developing nations around the world.

How did these sisters get to this place in their lives, to this business, and to this commitment? First, they had a great relationship with each other, based on trust, mutual respect, a shared childhood, and aligned values. Then they looked at their skills and visions.

Kelly always loved to travel. She worked for a number of years on the public relations side of the New York fashion industry, which involved a great deal of travel. She loved the local arts and crafts she would find on her trips, but she was not happy in the fashion industry. The hours alone were horrific, and she didn't feel her work mattered. Kelly says, "In my heart and soul, I wanted to work for something worthwhile."

Anne had a background in development and began to toss around the idea of socially responsible tourism. The sisters were inspired by their travels to send money to village cooperatives, and the idea grew from there. In fact, it snowballed.

Kelly and Anne work the business together, and they take travelers with them – about twenty on each trip – individuals who love to travel and who want to make a difference in these developing countries. The Village Experience is, in their words, "a socially proactive business dedicated to uplifting impoverished communities in the developing world through efforts in international trade and tourism."

The organization has two components: the first is global tourism, with the intent of providing the visitors a cultural education, a humanitarian experience, and a true adventure. All the trips give travelers a "real, off-the-beaten path" village experience. For some, education about developing countries would be enough, but not for Kelly and Anne. They want to promote self-sufficiency for the people in the communities their travelers visit, helping them overcome poverty, lack of education, and disease. That brings in the second component of The Village Experience: the nonprofit sector, which focuses broadly on international trade. They work with charities, micro-financing groups, women's projects, local artisans, and global cooperatives to stimulate business in the villagers' home communities, and to help the people create fair trade products that The Village Experience store promotes for them in the developed world.

Their store sells items like Kazuri beads made by Kenyan women, as well as handmade journals from Nepal, Zambian soap, banana leaf baskets, Thai wine bags, Indian batik silk

"The business snowballed as a result of our relationships. We create relationships everywhere we go."

and wool scarves, candles and candle holders, handbags, home décor, and bamboo bowls. All the goods are made in the communities the sisters visit and support. Their items are available online as well, further expanding the market for the artisans in these developing countries.

"The business snowballed as a result of our relationships. We create relationships everywhere we go. Locally, we promote awareness in the township schools. We reach out to people of all faiths, whether in their churches, synagogues, or mosques. We have been at National Geographic shows, gift fairs, in magazines, and we go out of our way to interact with any organization doing community outreach. In fact, our store has become a meeting place for people in nonprofits and congregations. It is like a museum of sorts. People gather to meet each other and exchange ideas.

"We also offer our store as a fundraising site: schools and organizations use our fair trade products to raise funds for their needs and initiatives." The store opened in September 2009 and already has a significant reputation in Indianapolis and beyond. A school looking for a cultural project need look no further than The Village Experience. Kids from grade school through college find incredible learning opportunities interwoven with a network that supports individuals and communities in need around the globe.

Kelly explains, "The for-profit sector foots the bill for the nonprofit sector. In addition, the trips cultivate a sense of commitment in the people who travel there. Hence, we have the 'Kenya project people,' for example; those who, as a result of their visit, are devoted to supporting Kenyan orphanages or helping start agricultural ventures there. Then when we learn of a group of villagers who want to start a new project, we approach these people for funding. Most projects involve very small investments, requiring just a few hundred dollars. It is so rewarding to see our small contributions make such a big difference in the lives of these people and their communities.

"Furthermore, we know that these fledgling businesses will improve the lives and education of their children. The benefit of this assistance will go on for years to come. The trip visitors are our best marketing tool, not only for future trips, but for the funding of these small business projects."

The Village Experience's traveler market is composed largely of college students. The trips stimulate their understanding of world culture, politics, and economics, while simultaneously teaching them about fundraising. Most students fundraise to earn the $2,000 cost of the trip – a low price for a two-week excursion to an exotic destination like Uganda or Thailand. Some students hit the bars and restaurants to raise money. They also hold parties in the store, doing whatever it takes to raise the funds they need. The students are powerfully moved by the difference they make on these expeditions, and the memories stay with them. Kelly and Anne simultaneously promote a sense of social responsibility in the people who make these trips as well as helping the communities they visit. As the business is so new, only time will tell how the impact of these excursions will affect the lives and work of these college students.

Earning money to make the trip is just the students' first learning experience. "When the visitors arrive," Kelly explains, "they must learn not to give handouts to the impoverished. The people hate to be given a few dollars out of charity." Instead, Kelly teaches, "Loan them your laptop so they can create and submit business proposals to The Village Experience. That is when the villagers get really excited," because they understand how these tools can help them become more self-sufficient and prosperous.

The initial projects are designed to produce food for the villagers' children and funds for their education. The additional income they generate is used to buy medicine and meet other daily needs, like fixing their homes. The money funds are circulated into their larger local community, enhancing lives there, too.

Additionally, the locals meet with others involved in the business startup process. They share ideas and expertise. "Folks from another village in Kenya went to see the chicken coop started in Mbita. They were so excited when they learned that they could do the same thing at home," Kelly says. Kelly and Anne have made the most of the Chinese saying, "Give a person a fish, you feed them for a day. Teach a person to fish, you feed them for a lifetime." The projects the sisters support not only feed one individual for a lifetime, but many.

Hearing about Kelly and Anne's work in Mbita is incredibly inspiring. To learn that it is but a small segment of the overall, far-reaching mission of The Village Experience is eye-opening. While in Kenya, Kelly and her travelers spent time with Alive and Kicking, a community-owned business that makes and sells soccer balls to raise money and awareness about HIV/AIDS. The Village Experience group purchased some balls to support the cause.

In Nakuru, a bus ride away, is one of many orphanages that house some of the millions of orphans that Kenya struggles to clothe, feed, house, and educate each year. The Child Discovery Center is home to approximately 100 exceptionally bright children. The travelers spent time engaging with these children, listening to their stories, laughing with them, and helping them with their crafts. They then went on to another orphanage, the Saidia Children's Home, where they donated the soccer balls they had purchased from Alive and Kicking. An impromptu soccer game broke out, after which the group planted trees with the children.

All along the way, the travelers experienced wildlife, local markets, and restaurants. They took every opportunity to get to know the local people – their smiles, their hardships, their needs, and their dreams. Quickly, the scope of The Village Experience's work moves from being merely inspiring to sincerely profound.

The Village Experience is bigger still than these worthy projects, as it supports other programs like Lords Mead, a rehabilitation center, vocational college, and secondary school for child soldiers and HIV/AIDS orphans in Uganda. The Seeds of Help Foundation provides assistance to people in the highlands of Guatemala. Thailand's Baan Tharn Namchai Orphanage helps orphans still suffering from the 2004 tsunami.

Perhaps the most remarkable aspect of the Campbell sisters' work is that they completed these goals in their first eighteen months of business. While they were developing relationships and engaging others to support their progress, they continued to strengthen their own relationship, which has clearly been the catalyst for their success.

Kelly and Anne's shared vision is to start one or two more stores so they can distribute their clients' fair trade products throughout the United States. They would like to offer trips to locations across the world and expand their current twelve annual trips to a trip a week for the whole year. Kelly adds, "I'd like to see the way we think about and distribute aid change. Handouts keep people entrenched in their current state of need. They need to be empowered by our dollars to develop businesses that will get them out of poverty and extinguish that need once and for all."

Kelly and Anne's dad was an entrepreneur. It is not surprising that Kelly's inspiration came from one of her closest relationships. As a child, she often thought it would only be a matter of time before she'd venture into entrepreneurship herself. Now that she's taken that plunge, she loves it. "It's a continual learning process," she says. Is it better than her other jobs? "It's not a job. It's a lifestyle." And she wouldn't trade it for anything else in the world.

For more information on Kelly and Anne Campbell and The Village Experience, visit experiencethevillage.com.

The Precious Nature of Relationships

Perhaps the most precious "thing" in life is our relationships with others – our family, friends, colleagues and coworkers, teachers and mentors, neighbors, and others in our communities. Frequently, when people are asked about their biggest regrets, at the top of the list are those concerning their relationships: parents regret not having spent more time with their children, sons and daughters regret the failure to repair their relationship with parents, people regret fights that destroyed marriages and friendships. This list is probably endless.

Dr. Joshua Haberman, founder of the Foundation for Jewish Studies, in his lecture "Illusions We Cherish," related how Dr. Karl Menninger, a prominent psychiatrist and founder of the Menninger Clinic, replied when asked what he would do if he felt a nervous breakdown coming on. Menninger answered, "Go across the street and help another person!" Haberman makes the point that we are "dependent upon others for significant relationships in which we recover our sense of purpose." While we may feel autonomous and self-reliant, our sense of value depends largely on who we can be for others – in our relationships.

Haberman refers to a character in a Lewis Carroll story, a jittery padlock with spidery arms and legs that always seems to be running to and fro. At one point in the story, another character approaches the padlock and asks, "What is the matter with you? Why are you so excited and unhappy?" The padlock replies, "I am seeking the key to unlock myself!"

Haberman observes, "Many of us are locked inside ourselves. We wonder about our purpose. What is our reason for existence? We go through life looking for the key to unlock life. And we never find it – because nobody has the key to his own life. We should be looking for it beyond ourselves, because the meaning of our life is disclosed to us only in our relationship to others."

Relationships are vital to the mission of unlocking our life and finding meaning. It is with, through, and for others that we realize who we are, discover our purpose, and become truly fulfilled. Yet building and maintaining relationships requires work and the investment of time, emotions, energy, thoughtfulness, and selfless behavior. We do, of course, benefit from our investment in relationships. The degree to which we experience this may vary with each individual's experiences; however, we generally receive many times more than what we put in overall. The benefits may seem intangible or even elusive at times, but they accumulate as we extend ourselves to others through our work, interests, and relationships.

Relationships Are a Mirror

Two of the most remarkable gifts of relationships are that they help us see who we are and discover who we would like to become. It is as if, when we look at another, we are really staring at a reflection of ourselves. Every time we experience a moment of deep love and connection with someone, we discover within us a wellspring of the best we can be. Every time we help, support, or uplift someone else, we see just how loving we can be.

Even in difficult moments, relationships can teach us. When we fight with someone we love, we can walk away committed to the idea that we were right (which, of course, means that the other person was wrong), or we can feel sadness about the break – however momentary – in the bond of that relationship. If we allow ourselves to experience the sadness, the argument can become a teachable moment; we can discover the potential to repair and prevent a similar situation in the future. We can use the disappointment to catapult us into a different way of responding when we feel strongly about something or when we are upset.

As is well demonstrated by Kelly and Anne through their partnership in The Village Experience, relationships are crucial to fulfilling our purpose in life. Every individual they meet offers a ray of light. So too, every person we encounter offers wisdom from which we can learn. Through this, we see more of who we are and we radiate more of our own light.

It is also through relationships that we express and practice living our values. We tell people what is important to us and demonstrate it through our actions and choices. One way we know we are effectively living our values is when people reflect and honor our values in their interactions with us. We also know we are effective when others begin modeling our values in their own lives. The goal, however, is not to get people to change for us; rather, it is to draw to us those who share the values we prize.

Think about how you engage in your relationships and nourish them. Do you consider how others respond to you? As aware as we may be about our need to nourish our relationships – especially those closest to our hearts – we all occasionally behave poorly, do things of which we are not proud, or contribute to unfortunate situations, even if unintentionally. We are blessed in that we can learn from our mistakes and that we have the ability to make amends. A sincerely offered apology, backed by our words and deeds, is among the most significant gestures we can make. This is often the first step toward healing wounded relationships.

Why does this matter? Because our self-respect is usually tied to the esteem of those whom we love most deeply, and we know that when we have done something to challenge that trust, we have compromised our own sense of safety and security. We have lost a piece of the very thing that makes us whole. Until we can reorient ourselves and get that relationship back on track, our world is not quite right.

What We Stand to Lose

A woman named Abby had a terrible argument with her father over an insensitive remark she made. She was upset over the incident and apologized to her father time and again, but he refused to accept her apologies, essentially cutting her out of his life. Abby and her husband have two children who are now young adults, and her father – their grandfather – hardly knew them. His unforgiving manner deprived him of these key relationships. Pride and anger caused him to forego the incredible joy and love he could have experienced with his grandchildren, the opportunity to add purpose and meaning through those relationships, as well as the possibility of enriching their lives. Abby's dad recently died, without ever accepting her apology or offering his forgiveness. What an unfortunate and unnecessary loss this was for both of them, as well as for all the others involved.

Unfortunately, Abby's story is not unique. So many relationships are destroyed or irreparably sacrificed on the altar of being right. Winning the argument or tenaciously trying to prove we are right – whether or not we are – often takes precedence over doing the right thing: solving the problem, working out the issue, or moving beyond our own bias. In our stubborn steadfastness, we risk losing the thing we most cherish – loving relationships with those who enrich our lives.

It's easy to allow little things to derail our efforts. Petty arguments can spiral out of control or we can choose to hold onto resentments, thinking we are punishing the other person or protecting ourselves from further hurt. Most likely, though, we are only hurting and depriving ourselves and the other person from all the satisfaction that restoring the relationship might bring.

It can be difficult to hear and thoughtfully consider the opinions, judgments, and choices of others who have different life experiences, perspectives, or assumptions about what is right. We often have an emotional investment in our own ideas, perceptions, and needs. Even as we may believe the common axiom that perception is reality, it is valuable to remember that others who have different perceptions may have different realities, and those differences may very well be the cause of many conflicts.

If we accept that our perceptions are our realities, it also may be helpful to explore why perceptions vary, and with them our nuggets of reality. This recognition is central to resolving differences more constructively and effectively. We can do this by acknowledging that:

- Our perceptions are influenced by our values, education, culture, experiences, beliefs, responsibilities, and position.

- Each of us has a different perception of what is true as a result of our different life experiences.

- Our use of language reflects our nuggets of reality.

- Our nuggets of reality are not the only ones on any given topic, and there can be more than one truth.

- Disagreements arise from conflicting perceptions, which affect our focus and our interpretations of conversations and events.

- We resolve conflicts and reach agreement when we constructively challenge each other's nuggets of reality and remain open to varying interpretations, assumptions, and conclusions. It is essential to understand and work through the source of our various perceptions.

Stepping back from our own perceptions of right and wrong and viewing situations through the eyes of others is a crucial step toward finding common ground, resolving conflicts, and restoring broken relationships. It requires an investment of time and effort, as well as an interest in tracing the differences back to the point from which our logic paths originally diverged.

A common business axiom says that it costs five times as much to win a new customer – in terms of time, effort, and money – than it does to retain a potentially dissatisfied customer. The same applies to our personal relationships. If we desire high-quality relationships, we must work to retain the ones we have – even when we hit rough patches.

Growing and Deepening Relationships

Repair of relationships is essential for our continuing growth and fulfillment. Equally important is the need to consistently deepen and expand our relationships. Sometimes our disappointment in developing, restoring, and maintaining relationships is not due to poor behavior on our part, but rather to our holding back. Perhaps we have not said something we really need to say. Maybe the circumstances require that we do something outside our comfort zone, like make the first step. To truly find the self-growth we are seeking, we must be willing to take the risk and have those scary and or uncomfortable conversations. They can bring a sense of life and vitality previously unimagined. It is our experience that when we are valued, our thoughts and feelings are valued as well.

INNER QUEST

Are there relationships that you would like to restore or repair?

OUTER QUEST

What can you do to take the first step?

Deepening and helping our relationships grow occurs through other means, as well. Are you married with children? When was the last time you had a date night with your spouse? Whether raising children or not, have you hit a point with your partner where you no longer speak intimately about subjects that matter to you? Do you consciously invest in your most valued relationships? It's essential that we all take regular time to nourish these relationships. By doing so, we find that they become more and more fulfilling as they become more intimate.

We have said a great deal about healing and expanding existing relationships, and how important both of these elements are to happiness and success in life. We have also discussed the impact relationships have on our personal growth. In addition to investing in our current relationships, extending ourselves to develop new relationships can be a crucial ingredient in enabling us to live our purpose and then realize our vision. For some, reaching out to meet new people is both joyful and easy. For others it may be difficult or uncomfortable. Just as we deepen the intimacy with our existing friends and loved ones, we can use the same skills to develop new connections. Doing so is enriching and will facilitate even greater progress along our journey.

Finding Meaning and Purpose through Connection

Relationships are not simply a tool for living a meaningful and purpose-enriched life; they are an integral part of the process. By enrolling others in our purpose, we can multiply the good we do and the number of lives we touch. Kelly and Anne exemplify this through The Village Experience. Kelly's purpose and vision depend on the relationships she forges with villagers around the world. The trust she develops strengthens her ability to help and empower the villagers. Relationships with universities and community groups are essential for the sisters to attract travelers to the countries and villages they support. Their store flourishes as a result of community and organizational relationships. Every step in The Village Experience is enhanced by relationships. The more relationships that Kelly and Anne create, nourish, and maintain, the greater their ability to fulfill their vision.

Maintaining enduring relationships like these requires a strong foundation that involves trust, honesty, empathic listening, and compassion. It requires that we truly care about the people with whom we are relating. If we establish relationships on false pretenses, by pretending to be someone we are not, our relationships will eventually wither, no matter how much we care about them. We need to be authentic about who and what we are, or eventually our own behavior will betray us. This is why values play such a key role, both while a relationship is developing and when it is mature.

Engaging Others

Along with values, relationships are at the core of our search for greater meaning and fulfillment, because our progress on our inner and outer journeys depends on others. Enjoining others to become involved in our purpose is essential to the meaning and fulfillment we seek. We refer to this process as "engaging others."

Think about the purpose you have begun to articulate. It likely includes others. You may have a vision for community involvement or a way of helping a certain group of people. The steps you take to realize your vision and purpose will necessitate interactions with others, and their levels of involvement will vary in degree. You may ultimately create and engage an entire community to help pursue your purpose, like Janice, an observant Lutheran, married to Seth, an observant Jew. While the couple chose to raise their children in the Jewish faith, Janice is quite committed to her own faith. Living as an interfaith couple, the family has had a great deal of exposure to the misunderstandings different faiths have about other faiths. Janice therefore finds interfaith dialogue extremely important.

> For ambitious undertakings, your success may hinge on how well you rally others to your vision.

As director of the children's choir at her church, Janice recently forged a relationship between the sixth grade children in her congregation and those of her husband's synagogue. She wanted the Lutheran children to experience a Jewish Sabbath service. She taught the children in both communities melodies they could sing together. The children and their families attended the service, as did the larger congregations. The children and families exchanged rituals, shared traditions, and made many new friends. The experience was such a success that it was repeated the following year, continuing the community-building. While Janice is doing her small piece to create relationships between these two faith communities, she recognizes that she needs the support and cooperation of both of the participating organizations in order to succeed.

Anne and Kelly do a similar thing each day in The Village Experience. Their travelers are one community they engage; the villagers another; school children and religious organizations, others still. The act of engaging others is imbued with great beauty, because we can see directly how our work positively affects their lives.

Another example of engaging communities is demonstrated by the counselors, support staff, and campers who participate in Camp Swift, described in Chapter 2, "The Journey to Find Meaning and Become a 'Heartisan.'" Each of these communities comes together to make a difference: the counselors and support staff to serve and the campers to receive, yet all are strengthened in the end.

There is another, very practical arm to engaging others. The larger our vision, the greater our need to involve others. This occurs for two reasons. First, a large vision, such as educating a community about an illness, like Denise Resnik's, or repairing an injustice in the world, like Zuhdi Jasser's, involves teaching people to understand your goals so that they want to jump on board. The more people with whom you share your vision, the more who will work with you to achieve those goals. As greater numbers of people become aligned with your purpose, more of them will be likely to help you pursue it. For ambitious undertakings, your success may hinge on how well you rally others to your vision.

The second reason engaging others is important relates to the need for specific skills to fulfill your vision. Take a moment to think about Carolyn Manning and the Welcome to America Project. As much as Carolyn resisted the idea of asking people for help, she knew she needed their support and expertise to achieve her goals. Each person she engaged helped her move forward, from helping that first family, to birthing WTAP, to expanding it into the organization it is today.

Making progress in any arena requires certain strengths, knowledge, and talents, some of which you possess and some that others possess. You must know your own strengths and weaknesses, and be able and willing to engage people with the skills and abilities that are not your strong suit. Developing this capacity, along with the energy, ideas, and esprit de corps that springs from a motivated team, will enable you to accelerate your progress dramatically.

Building a team is just one form of engaging others. There are many other ways, all of which can work together, with none being mutually exclusive. For example, your purpose might be similar to Dov Vogel's, the hospital clown you met in Chapter 3, "Where to Begin," who finds fulfillment in entertaining patients. To fulfill such a purpose, you would need to engage the hospital staff for permission and set up a schedule. You might want to engage businesses to donate products for use in your entertainment. Eventually, you might even want to involve other people in doing the same work so you could touch more children. Of course, you would be engaging the patients you entertained, and you would want their feedback to make sure you were meeting their needs. Each of these is an example of engaging others which, in turn, would help you advance your goal.

Your vision might be of a grand scale, either local or on the other side of the world. For a grand vision, you will likely need to engage others in myriad roles. You might need someone who is great with numbers; perhaps an artist or a designer; you might need people to collect donations, make phone calls, raise funds, or work side-by-side with you; someone

> "In everyone's life, at some time, our inner fire goes out. It is then burst into flame by an encounter with another human being. We should all be thankful for those people who rekindle the inner spirit."
> — Albert Schweitzer

might be in charge of publicity and communication. Each of these areas requires a certain expertise, so connecting with knowledgeable people in each field is crucial. You might have a need to organize people into teams or committees. Depending on the size and scope of your vision, the variety of skills and number of people you need to engage may be quite significant. By enrolling in your vision with their individual gifts and expertise, they can become an additional support system as you proceed on your LifePath.

A powerful vision is often surrounded by supporters – numbers of people who believe in the vision and work toward making it a reality. One reason is that the vision has been clearly articulated and resonates with many people who turn out to support it. Another is that they believe in the integrity of those sharing the vision. Finally, big visions attract those who are aligned in their thinking and thus are willing to work to realize the dream. Once a critical mass of people is engaged in an idea or behavior, it seems to take on a life of its own.

Whom to Engage: The Specifics

Engaging others in your vision and purpose can move it forward faster and more robustly than you could move it along on your own steam. If this is your goal, the next logical question becomes, "Whom can I invite along on this journey?" To answer this question, you must identify the qualities you are seeking in supporters. For example:

- Skills, knowledge, or expertise that supplements your own and will strengthen your endeavors
- Relevant experience
- Passion or interest in the cause
- Values similar to or compatible with yours
- A vision that is aligned with yours
- Helpful relationships and contacts
- Resources (e.g., time, money, equipment)
- Personal compatibility with you and the others on your team
- Openness to working collaboratively and cooperatively

Our ability to engage others effectively is closely tied to how we relate to others and how well we communicate our vision. The better our relationship skills overall, the better we are able to engage the right people to help us achieve our vision. We must be ready and willing to always see the best in each person, remembering that even under stress, these others are our allies and are committed to the same results.

Engaging others begins by sharing your vision with them and ensuring that they see it clearly. Once they are on board, the next step is to make sure that everyone is moving in the same direction to support the endeavor. Once you are sure they are aligned with your goals, you must help the others find the proper roles in the process and see clearly how their roles contribute to the overall success of the mission. It is important for them to develop their own sense of ownership in your vision.

People who are involved in a common undertaking tend to be more motivated and aligned when they understand the connection between their work and the ultimate objectives. This enhances the overall effectiveness in achieving the goal. Their passion joins with yours to create greater power and momentum. This concept is referred to as "line-of-sight." Communicating the importance of this connection and helping people see how everything fits together is a critical leadership responsibility.

Acknowledgment

Because the people in our lives, whether personal relationships or simply those we meet along our LifePath, have feelings, they need to know that who they are and what they do makes a difference to us. When someone goes the extra mile for us at home – perhaps your child makes you breakfast or your spouse gets around to that honey-do list – a thank you is incredibly important. Beyond the words themselves is recognition of their contribution.

People engaged with us in our vision may be working against long odds, on a tight timeline, with scant materials, or simply investing a great deal of themselves. It's very important to acknowledge them for what they bring to the effort – this recognition helps them feel valued and appreciated. It also fuels their respect and loyalty, and fosters their continued desire to engage with you in the project. This type of recognition can be offered one-on-one or as a team, though it is believed that praise offered in front of others has a much more profound effect on the receiver. Either way, people who feel valued in their work will give you their best effort and often be your best supporters.

Engage a Mentor or Coach

Among the most important people we recommend engaging is a mentor and/or coach. A mentor is a knowledgeable, and hopefully wise, counselor and advisor. This individual (and you may have more than one) should be someone in whom you can confide and trust. A coach is your "go to" person when you need sage insight or advice about approaching a challenge, someone who will help you think through matters and guide you on an action plan to enhance your success.

You may find that you need a mentor and a coach, or that you have a stronger need for one or the other. Your mentor and coach could be one and the same. On the other hand, you may find it valuable to have multiple perspectives and teachers, depending on the situation. The essential things are understanding the kind of support you need, and that the person or people you select have the capabilities, experience, judgment, and integrity you require. You must, of course, be able to trust them.

NAVIGATIONAL POINTS

- Relationships are vital to living a meaningful life.
- Relationships require an investment and nourishment.
- Repair of damaged relationships is essential to our well-being and fulfillment.
- Relationships are precious and can be irreparably harmed if we do not take steps to heal them when they are broken.
- Deepening our relationships adds richness and fulfillment for all involved.
- Expanding our circle of relationships is essential to our growth and to the growth of our vision.
- Successful relationships rely on trust and our ability to live our values, day to day.
- Engaging others effectively, whether on a large or small scale, is central to the effective pursuit of our purpose.
- Plan who you will engage and how, to ensure the creation of an effective team with the skills you need.

- Effective communication nourishes relationships
- Express how much you value each individual, and connect each person's contribution to your objectives – creating a clear line of sight.
- Seek help from a mentor and/or coach to enhance your success.
- Acknowledge the people in your home life and on your LifePath for the well-being of all.

APPLYING THE CONCEPTS TO YOUR LIFE

1. What are three or four words you'd like others to use when describing the kind of person they know you to be?

2. Identify your key relationships. Indicate the following about each of them:
   - How fulfilling is the relationship?
   - How would you like to improve the relationship?
   - What are some action steps you can take to improve the relationship?

3. Identify key individuals who might help you achieve your vision (either by name, job description, organizational affiliation, etc.). Indicate the following about each of them:
   - What special skills or knowledge would they bring to your vision?
   - What are steps you can take to meet/engage them in your vision?
   - What is your timeline for meeting/engaging them?

For worksheets and additional exercises on developing healthy relationships and engaging others, visit FindFulfillFlourish.com; then click on Book & Tools.

Chapter 8

Living Possibilities: Making the Impossible Possible

Believing in your purpose

Positive thinking and messaging

Overcoming challenges to bring your purpose to life

Lifting Women as They Build New Lives: Elaine Birks-Mitchell and The Bra Recyclers

A woman runs from her house in the middle of the night, grabbing her kids and rushing them into the car before her enraged husband can get to them. She knows the way to the shelter. Though she's thought about leaving before, she never has. She's driven by a number of times, just checking it out. Her friends keep telling her to leave, advising her to go there. The idea's been simmering for some time, yet every time she seriously considered leaving her husband, he seemed to get better. She wanted to believe he wouldn't hit her anymore, just like he promised, but then the drinking would start again, and the words were as thin as air.

His fists, though, are real – hard and thick and extremely heavy, as they hit her arms, her torso, her face. This time truly is the last time, and not because her husband said so, but because this time he has gone too far. This time she sees her little daughter race across the room as her husband charges at her. She sees the fear in her little girl's eyes – her beautiful, sweet, innocent daughter – and something gives. In a split second, she sees her daughter as a grown woman being beaten, and she realizes that she has to get out now.

Once her husband conks out, following his good drunk and wild rage, she slips out of the bedroom as quietly as she can, quickly and noiselessly gathering her three children and shushing them with her finger to her lips. She packs them into the car, praying her husband will remain passed out long enough for them to get away. Easing out of the driveway without so much as a breath, in fear of making any noise, she backs out, puts the car in drive, and turns onto the street. As soon as she gets past the corner, she turns the headlights on and tears off.

Her next memory is waking to both solace and fear: relief that she is away from her abuser and in a supportive environment, fear about what to do next. What will she tell the children? How will she care for them? Where will they live? Now, all the familiar things in her life are gone. Looking down, she realizes that the only clothing she has is what she is wearing, a nightie and a robe. She doesn't have any other clothes for herself or her children.

The women at the shelter help with this, providing her with a couple of outfits and some clothes for the children to wear. After she has the kids settled in school, the shelter's next step is to help her get back on her feet, which includes therapy and career counseling.

Within a short time she has a couple of job interviews. The shelter has a re-lationship with a nonprofit organization that supplies business clothes for women just like her, and she is able to find a suit that matches the color of her eyes and fits her elegantly. Then, once again, she is reminded of the panic in which she fled her house – in her nightclothes, she hadn't even packed a toothbrush, let alone a bra. It would feel odd, disrespectful, even a bit slimy, to attend her interviews without proper support. The thought tears at her already fragile self-esteem. But where will she find a bra?

* * *

Enter The Bra Recyclers, an organization dedicated to providing bras for women in need. At first glance, this may seem like a silly sort of business, but as founder Elaine Birks-Mitchell explains, the need is quite widespread and deeply significant.

Elaine poses the following scenario: Surely you've cleaned out your closet and given away a pile of clothing to the Salvation Army or a homeless shelter. The bags are full of old dresses, pants, and sweaters you don't wear anymore – and then, of course, there are last year's shoes. Someone will be able to use them.

But what about your bras? If you are like many women, your mom told you that you can give anything away to those in need, except underwear. Those, she might have told you, go into the trash. But if you pause to think about it, if there is a need for your old pants and tops, isn't there also a need for your old bras?

Elaine asked this exact question when she was cleaning out her closet a few years ago. Raised in a family that taught her to think about others and focus on giving back, she reflected on these kinds of questions from time to time. This particular time, her reflection led to a brainstorm that could only be borne from living in possibility.

Elaine had worked in the information technology field for twenty years. She regularly put in twelve-hour days or longer, simply because that was what the job required. It was great for paying the bills, but one day, she simply got tired. In 2005, she quit her job. A year later, an unexpected job opportunity moved her to Phoenix. She worked with the new company for a year, until she realized she was doing essentially the same work as before, just in a new location. She again felt burned out and decided to move on.

Then, a synchronicity of events took place in Elaine's life. After cleaning her closet and wondering what to do with the bras she could no longer wear, she saw a segment on television about the bra manufacturing process. Elaine learned that the making of these garments is filled with time-consuming detail and expensive materials. With today's emphasis on conserving resources, Elaine thought, "There must be a way to recycle bras!"

Elaine began to think about women who are victims of domestic violence, and she wondered about their circumstances. She knew women in her own life who had either been in abusive, unhealthy, or unloving relationships, so it was a natural leap to think about women's shelters. She called a local shelter and asked: "Would you have a need for recycled bras?" Elaine received an overwhelming and resounding response of "YES!" and The Bra Recyclers was born.

The Bra Recyclers has two facets that work hand-in-hand. One side is a nonprofit, and the other a for-profit business. The mission of the nonprofit side is:

> To enhance the lives of deserving women by providing them with re-cycled bras and to build an international bra recovery and recycling program that:
>
> 1. Raises community awareness about the importance of recovering and recycling bras.

2. Becomes an advocate for deserving women of all ages who struggle with obtaining the basic needs to live, including something as simple as a bra.

3. Provides an easy way for women to support other deserving women by recycling their used and unused bras.

The for-profit arm enhances the potential and possibilities of the nonprofit arm. Elaine discovered she could sell recycled bras to international exporters for a profit, and use the income to fund her bra donation efforts. Oddly enough, even though the export segment is for-profit, Elaine learned that it, too, provides a much needed service: many women in developing cities and countries in Russia, South America, and Africa now have access to bras, when they previously did not. Elaine learned that some African women have been buying lots of the used bras, opening stores, and reselling them to local women. Not only is this meeting a need for bras, but it is boosting the local economy in those areas while creating new business opportunities and steady incomes for entrepreneurial women. In her desire to support women, Elaine finds this unexpected benefit deeply rewarding.

Elaine is committed to offering a minimum of 10 percent of her bra inventory each year as a donation. She took this number from her religious texts, where she learned that tithing means offering 10 percent of one's income to those in need. Many of the donated bras go to women in domestic violence shelters, just like the woman in the opening story of this chapter. Unfortunately, this situation is all too common. The details of each story may be different, but the pattern is eerily similar.

Stories like this cannot help but touch our hearts. Shockingly, the percentage of women who report experiencing some form of violence in an intimate relationship is as high as one in three. Relatively few of these women actually seek refuge in shelters, but for those who do, Elaine's willingness to create new possibilities through small but emotionally significant donations helps empower these women to live lives of their own choosing, free of violence. Then they, too, can live in possibility.

Elaine creates a special relationship with each shelter to which she

> "The reasonable man adapts himself to the conditions that surround him. The unreasonable man adapts surrounding conditions to himself. All progress depends on the unreasonable man."
> — George Bernard Shaw

donates. They place orders for the specific bra sizes they need, so that the women can be appropriately fitted. This simple yet fundamental contribution helps these women maintain their dignity and restore their self-respect while they rebuild their lives. "To step out into a job interview," Elaine explains, "women need to be properly supported. Having a recycled bra offered to them is a true self-esteem booster that helps them dress for success."

Elaine sees the need for bras as a metaphor for the need for women's empowerment in other areas, as well. For example, runaway pre-teens desperately need help to shift their lives in a healthy direction. Therefore, another recipient of Elaine's bras is Florence Crittenton, an organization that helps girls as young as eleven years old to get off the street. Elaine donated bras to these young girls last year, and plans to continue to support them in the coming years.

Where do these bras come from? They come from Elaine's friends, people like you and me, and also from interesting, unexpected places. Sloan-Kettering Hospital in New York City is one of the best known cancer hospitals in the country. Many women, unfortunately, visit as mastectomy patients. Post-mastectomy, some may have reconstructive surgery, while many others realize they can no longer use their current bras. Many of these women now donate those bras to The Bra Recyclers. In another case, a gentleman in California contacted Elaine directly after his wife passed away. He was going through her things and wanted to donate them to worthy causes. He learned about The Bra Recyclers, and donated his wife's bras to the organization.

Elaine also solicits donations directly from bra manufacturers. While some choose to donate, Elaine learned, sadly, that most bras the manufacturers don't sell wind up in landfills. What a terrible waste, especially when they could be worn by women who really need them but can't afford them.

In 2009, Elaine completed her first full year of business. Her goal was to collect and distribute 10,000 bras. She doubled that, gathering and distributing more than 20,000 of these essential garments. She provided donations to ten facilities serving women who are either homeless, escaping domestic violence, or pre-teen runaways. Now in her second year, Elaine's goal is to provide twenty facilities with bras. As she continues to contact more facilities, she discovers just how expansive the need is. Her long-term goal is to ensure that every domestic violence shelter in the United States has bras to offer women, who, in her words "need a lift."

"At the end of the day," Elaine says, "I'm tired, but excited. It is a different kind of tired than I experienced while working in the IT business." Today, she puts in thirty to forty hours each week, in addition to holding a full-time job. But when you look at Elaine's face, it sparkles. Her smile of radiance and joy is the first thing you see. Elaine is doing work that makes her happy because it provides a service that is so basic and so necessary.

Asked why she chose this work, she says, "I always had a passion for supporting women and children. I always loved children. I was in a field for so many years with very few women, and I have always been interested in seeing women succeed. I had this passion; I just didn't know how to put it into action. I finally decided I wanted to do something on my own. Inside, I said, *I know I can.* I found this niche market and just ran with it. It provides women with a way to give in this tight economy without costing them too much. All they need to do is clear out a drawer."

Elaine has big plans. She again emphasizes, "There should be no shelter in this country that does not have bras." That would be a tremendous accomplishment. In addition, though, she wants to inspire women in the corporate world who want to give back. She is thinking of setting up branches around the country, and she may write a book. However, anyone who runs a franchise of The Bra Recyclers, in Elaine's words, "has to be a special person. Their goal must be to help people transition back into the community, rather than simply to make money. The money is secondary." Earning, she tells us, is a cycle: "The more you give back, the more you receive. You have to spend money to make money. The same is true with giving of your heart."

Once again, with a broad smile on her face, Elaine says, "I do this because it's what you should do." While it may be easy for Elaine to give back because it is such an integral part of her LifePath, the arena in which she chose to do so is unusual. It takes a very creative mind to find a use for something that so many people consider trash. It requires ingenuity to imagine a business centered around providing bras to women whose lives are torn or fractured. It takes a constant willingness to believe in possibilities. The very idea of recycling bras may cause some to feel embarrassed or uncomfortable, but not Elaine. She has found a way to reuse an expensive, intimate article of clothing to help women rebuild their self-esteem and success.

To learn more about The Bra Recyclers, visit brarecycling.org.

Living Possibilities and a Purposeful Life

Living a positive, meaningful life requires focusing on what you want to create. We are all products of our past – our life experiences, education, successes, setbacks, the values we learn as children, and the influential people in our lives. You may have been nourished with positive reinforcement and resources to help create meaning and fulfillment in your life, or you may have been instilled with a set of beliefs that emphasize limitation, fear, anger, and diminished self-esteem. Our success or failure is often determined by how we build on fortuitous situations – and rebound from bad ones.

Perhaps your environment gave you some of the positive and some of the negative. The influence of your past experiences can help optimize your potential or serve to limit you. Ideologies and skills you inherited or learned along the way serve as a point of departure for your actions. Whatever the current shape and composition of your platform today, you can decide how to use it going forward: to keep you stuck, or as a springboard that propels you into a positive, meaningful, and fulfilling future.

If you were raised with focused attention on designing your life for maximum value, your foundation is probably already strong. If you were not – and it's likely that most of us are in this category – chances are good that your foundation is laced with trap doors and weak planks over which you keep tripping, beliefs and behaviors that keep you stuck in your past. The cost of maintaining these paradigms and beliefs, no matter how comforting or safe they may feel, is a less rewarding today and a tomorrow that falls short of your desires. You may be unintentionally creating a future that closely resembles your present; therefore, one of the most important challenges is to release self-limiting thoughts and behaviors so that you can break through to a more fulfilling future.

Why are we still so affected by the experiences from our past? How do they continue to inhibit us from being who we want to be right now? Some people learn patterns in childhood that, often out of necessity, help them endure uncomfortable, difficult, or even abusive situations. When we learned those behaviors, they were essential for our survival. However, as we mature and develop our independence, we no longer need those survival behaviors; yet because they have become habit, we find ourselves continuing to engage in them long after the threat is gone and they no longer serve us. We carry that once-useful defense against a hurtful individual or experience into the present and future. That tiny, yet loud, self-limiting voice lives on inside us, and we keep responding to it long after it has served its purpose. Now, instead of being a tool for survival, it has become an obstacle to our well-being and fulfillment.

We may allow the negative experiences from our past to tax our present and future, limiting our ability to succeed. For example, we may hold grudges, remaining focused on intended or unintended slights, or the sense of being wronged or cheated. To move forward in our lives, we must first recognize that our choices are holding us back; then we need to learn to leave the issues of the past in the past, where they belong. Only then can we refocus on designing and living the life we desire, which can bring untold rewards.

If you feel stuck in a rut that continues to hold you back, limiting your ability to see and pursue new possibilities, the first step is to give yourself permission to change – permission to leap over the walls of the rut and view the horizon. Allow yourself to seek ways to alter your perspective and connect with positive people who are practiced at seeing possibilities. Optimism, belief in an exhilarating future, and positive thinking can be contagious.

Many of us are fortunate to meet a friend or mentor who helps us climb out of our self-limiting patterns. What a gift! But they're not available 24/7, and they are not always available in the way we may want or need them to be. The good news is that, like Elaine, we can be our own resource for transforming our lives. In order to do this, we must learn to tap into our own sense of optimism and create positive energy. These will then become drivers of our innovation, creativity, and manifestation.

The ability to remain focused and to retain our belief in new possibilities is key, especially when faced with the skepticism of others, setbacks, and disappointments. Success or failure is often determined by how well we build on good breaks and rebound from bad ones. Persistence and tenacity are essential to your success.

John is one such example of focus, tenacity, and positive thinking. He is Caucasian, living in a multi-ethnic community with his Korean wife and their adopted African-American child. This is an individual whose idea of family is very inclusive of possibilities. Merging multiple ethnicities in his family, John learned first-hand about the hurtful acts people commit out of prejudice and ignorance. As a teacher, he realized that through education and sharing stories, people can overcome their biases about others who are different from them. John approached his church about starting a monthly program to address these differences in an open, caring forum. John's embrace of differences and possibilities motivates him to continue investing in this constructive program.

The Power of Words

Think about the word *try*. Try with all of your might to turn the page without moving your hand. Now think about your results. Did you achieve anything in this experiment of *trying*?

Now think about the word *do*. Do something right now. Lift your hand and turn the page of the book. Set the book down and open the window shade near your chair to let in some light. Did you achieve different results with this experiment in *doing*? Trying is theoretical. Doing gets results.

Try is a word with little power. Similar to a self-limiting pattern of behavior, trying alone gets us nowhere. The concept of trying is a passive message, which, if we allow it to – and quite frequently we do – can become an excuse for halfhearted effort or giving up entirely. It may fuel a tendency to procrastinate or rationalize inaction or insignificant progress. "Well, I tried. I guess it just didn't work out." Doing is necessary for forward movement and achievement, ultimately taking us to new places and allowing us to explore new possibilities.

Other passive words include *wish* and *hope*. Like try, they tend to reflect a noncommittal state of mind, one in which we easily avoid responsibility for our lack of action or results. Living possibilities, on the other hand, is all about responsibility and accountability, to ourselves and to others who are relying on us for energetic and purposeful action. Possibilities are realized only through sustained action toward measurable goals.

We must always strive to use words that open up possibilities and drive us forward. Active words like *do, call, write, demonstrate, make, create,* and *produce*, for example, set us in motion and help us get beyond any limiting self-talk. When we hear ourselves using passive words such as *try, wish, want,* or *hope*, it's important to immediately restate these thoughts in active terms: replace the passive word with an active term that impels you to move forward.

Your success will largely depend on your ability to monitor your language and make a conscious effort to use active words and phrases. But it's not just about the word choices – you must also fortify your words with specific actions. Consider the words in the columns below and the commitment they reflect.

STATE OF MIND	STATE OF ACTION
Wish	Act
Hope	Do
Think	Follow through
Desire	Form
Want	Plan
Try	Create
Attempt	Perform
Intend	Develop
Imagine	Make
Consider	Establish
Look into	Prepare
Long for	Demonstrate
Dream	Drive

States of mind cannot be directly observed and therefore make it easy to excuse insufficient progress. Observable actions, on the other hand, produce outcomes and measurable progress toward goals.

Destructive Words

Just as we can create with words, we also have the power to immobilize ourselves with words. Two of the most immobilizing words in the English language are *I can't*. Some of the most destructive messages we send ourselves and others begin with *I can't*. However, often *I can't* is simply an excuse. When people use these words, what they frequently mean is: *I don't want to, I am unwilling to, It's just too much effort,* or *I won't.* They can also mean: *I don't know how* or *I am afraid to.*

We limit our own possibilities for achievement when we feed ourselves these kinds of self-defeating messages. The worst part is that we may even come to believe them before testing their accuracy or truth. They may inhibit our inclination to stretch ourselves, explore the art of the possible, or discover ways to overcome the challenges of making the impossible possible.

Ask yourself: *Do I really want to achieve this goal?* If the answer is a resounding Yes! then it's time to look at any concerns you might have: Do you need more education or experience? Do you need to engage someone else with know-how in a particular area? Are you afraid?

Many of us feel anxious when embarking on the unknown or when challenging our old belief systems. However, instead of letting these feelings overwhelm you with fear, these feelings can be your friend, guiding you to make healthy and wise choices. They can act as your advisor, encouraging you to bite off only as much as you can chew at any particular moment. Other times, your anxieties may simply voice acknowledgement of your trepidation; they do not have to become an excuse for not acting. You must work through your anxiety to quell it, and one of the best ways to alleviate it is by taking action. Once you begin to act, you may feel your anxieties evaporate or diminish greatly, especially when your adrenaline kicks in and you begin to see results from your actions.

Connection to Finding Meaning and Purpose

Focusing on and pursuing possibilities involves having a vision of what you can create or achieve in your life. It requires that you believe in what is possible and set realistic and stretch goals for achieving it. A realistic goal is easy to understand; it is a goal you know you are able and have the means to achieve. A stretch goal seems to be just out of reach; accomplishing it may require you to challenge yourself more than usual. This goal is achievable, if ambitious, but it will probably

When Robin studied dance in college, she had an extraordinary teacher, Gladys Bailin, a well-known modern dancer. Gladys was a small-but-mighty powerhouse, an invincible presence whether teaching technique or composition. One element of composition, also known as choreography, is improvisation. To become proficient, a dancer must do it often.

But art, like life, is filled with the unexpected. Occasionally, a dancer would slip, a leotard would tear, or instead of a beautiful lift, two people would collide. At these times, Gladys would yell, "Use it!" She would implore her students, no matter what the moment, to find a way to turn the experience – even something ridiculous or unthinkable – into something valu-

take more effort, greater skill, and perhaps a little luck to pull off. Stretch goals make realistic goals seem more doable because they set our sights higher and push us to exceed the status quo. Even if we do not reach our stretch goals, we may still exceed our expectations and create additional momentum. A stretch goal reflects your belief in possibilities.

For our realistic and stretch goals to be meaningful, they must have significance and value for you or others. For a goal to be purposeful, it must first have a reason to be achieved – whether it's meeting a need, accomplishing an objective, or creating something new and worthwhile for others. These are essential ingredients in a personal quest for fulfillment. We cannot achieve meaning and fulfillment by focusing only on ourselves. We must direct our search and efforts toward issues, causes, and visions beyond ourselves. In so doing, we can transform our inspirations and ideas into tangible things. We might even find ourselves embarking on quirky, atypical ideas, as Elaine Birks-Mitchell did. Regardless of how offbeat the idea, it's crucial that we give ourselves permission to think creatively and follow our hearts.

The search for meaning exists within you and outside of you; it is achievable by channeling your creative drive and allowing your imagination free reign.

Values

Our personal values are also crucial ingredients in our search for meaning. We are true to ourselves when our actions in life advance and reflect these values.

able. Her approach produced results on many levels. Her students learned that life has a flow, and that regardless of the events, we have an obligation to maintain that flow. The students' job was to make the dance seamless, even when the unexpected occurred. This is a valuable lesson to keep in mind when life hands us one of those unplanned, perhaps even unwanted, moments. When we see them as part of the flow, they will be less likely to force us off track.

Another result was that it taught the students to approach every moment as one of inspiration. Applying Gladys' philosophy to life beyond the dance studio can turn the planned and unplanned moments in our lives into things both of beauty and of practical value.

When our actions conflict with our values, we may experience anxiety or find our achievements devoid of meaning. This frequently occurs when we do things that are expedient rather than genuine. It also happens when we rationalize our actions by claiming that the ends justify the means. When our lives and goals reflect our deeply held values, we create more meaningful possibilities.

Once again, Elaine Birks-Mitchell's example is instructive. Elaine was raised with the core value of the importance of giving back. Her father taught her, "It's what you *should* do." Elaine's personal passion was to support women and children; she loves the idea of seeing women succeed. Elaine also has a strong sense of commitment. Together, these values guided her as she chose her LifePath, and they continue to inform her choices as she moves forward on that path.

INNER QUEST

Where are you on your path to create a new and better future than would otherwise exist without YOUR vision, YOUR action, and YOUR determination?

OUTER QUEST

What can you do today to make your life more closely resemble your vision?

Making the Impossible Possible

More often than we might imagine, seemingly impossible things are actually quite possible. Think about certain modern inventions that were once unimagined or considered not only impossible, but the stuff of fantasy novels: space travel, personal computers, the Internet, electronic books, cell phones, tiny cameras that enter the body on the end of a needle, to name only a few.

In the early 1800s, no one could have imagined that electricity might be harnessed and used to produce light, not to mention the millions of other items now powered by it. Thomas Edison is credited with inventing the electric light bulb in 1879, and it has transformed how we have lived ever since. He believed in what was possible and was driven to make it happen.

Likewise, the Wright Brothers are credited with inventing the first airplane, when most people believed human flight was impossible. In 1903, they successfully launched the first stable-wing aircraft. They believed, in spite of all odds, that their vision was possible, and they strove to bring it to life.

Believe it or not, as recently as ninety years ago, American women were forbidden to vote. In 1848, Elizabeth Cady Stanton and Lucretia Mott began a seventy-year struggle to obtain this right for women, a struggle that continued with intermittent successes and failures. Finally, their goal was fully realized in 1920, when Congress and President Woodrow Wilson granted American women this right with the passage of the 19th Amendment. Elizabeth and Lucretia did not live to see that historic day, but both believed that it would happen. They engaged the hearts and minds of others who continued their work after they were gone, eventually seeing it through to completion.

Edison, the Wright Brothers, Stanton and Mott all believed in possibilities that others could not envision. They were ridiculed, even labeled insane, because their visions stretched conventional thinking at the time. Living in possibilities allows you to envision your dream, even if you are its lone champion. Consider some of the dreams people have today that have not yet been realized: widespread peace; mass-produced and economical renewable energy; safe living conditions for all; remedies for currently incurable illnesses; clean air, food, and water across the globe; and peaceful religious coexistence. You may feel any number of these are unrealistic. And in our lifetimes, they may be. Yet striving to make even minimal progress toward any of them will affect myriad lives in a positive way – and little by little, the tangible results will become evident.

It's hard to know how far along other such visions of the future may be, whether they are grandiose, idealistic, ambitious, modest, or personal. However, when we focus on the possibilities and strive to create a better future, dreams begin to come true – even if they are only in our tiny corner of the world. But what an excellent starting point, our own place in the world! If Edison, in his frustration, had declared, "This is impossible!" the electric light bulb may not have been invented until much later, delaying all the breakthroughs it made possible. If the Wright Brothers had listened to conventional wisdom, they would not have pioneered flight. If Elizabeth Cady Stanton and Lucretia Mott hadn't worked tirelessly for women's suffrage, and inspired so many others to take up the cause after them, it is possible that American voting booths would still be used only by men. If Elaine Birks-Mitchell had been embarrassed to discuss the need for bras in women's shelters, 20,000 fewer bras would have been provided to needy women last year.

Possibility: believing that anything is feasible – *especially* that which you think is unattainable – is the key to transforming our world. Belief in possibilities brings the kind of fulfillment that validates your commitment and devotion to a life well-lived.

Getting There

To live our values in the process of achieving possibilities requires practice. We must practice the thought processes, behaviors, skills, and determination necessary to live the purpose-enriched life we seek – and ultimately to develop our full meaning and fulfillment. Malcolm Gladwell, in his bestselling book, *Outliers*, provides example after example of the importance of practice. His research shows that ten thousand hours of practice – roughly equivalent to five years of full-time work – is required to become truly proficient or develop great expertise in an area. It is essential that you continually practice the behaviors and thought processes necessary to achieve the possibilities you envision if you intend to manifest them. Practice is the difference between a dream and a dream realized.

> Practice is the difference between a dream and a dream realized.

Lewis Carroll in *Through the Looking Glass* makes this point in his unique way through this exchange between Alice and the Queen:

> *Alice laughed, "There's no use trying," she said. "One can't believe impossible things."*

> *"I daresay you haven't had much practice," said the Queen. "When I was your age, I always did it for half-an-hour a day. Why, sometimes I've believed as many as six impossible things before breakfast."*

Realistic Expectations

In today's world of instant communications, high-speed technology, and fast-paced change, it is easy to lose patience when progress toward attaining our goals is not immediate. However, most visions require the persistent belief in what is possible even in the face of formidable challenges, as well as the resilience to overcome setbacks. They often require continual effort over an extended period. Complex or chronic challenges generally require more than instant solutions. Idealism is important, tempered by the understanding that seemingly instant remedies usually do not resolve the root cause of issues. This point is discussed further in Chapter 11, "Passion to Action to Fruition."

As you continue to achieve your possibilities, remind yourself to maintain your idealism while keeping your expectations realistic. Big possibilities most often are achieved incrementally, rather than in one huge leap or breakthrough. Remaining positive and focused, even in the face of many frustrations, is the key to success. The self-fulfillment we all seek may be all the sweeter when the goals contain just a hint of impossibility.

NAVIGATIONAL POINTS

- Your life experiences are your springboard for propelling you into a meaningful and fulfilling future.
- Releasing limiting ideas, beliefs, and emotions will move your life and vision forward; replace them with action steps.
- Words create our reality: use positive, action-based words that reflect possibility and affirm your values.
- Use the unexpected and unplanned events in your life advantageously.
- Believe, like Edison and the Wright Brothers, that the impossible is possible.
- Stay open to novel ideas, unconventional thinking, and different perspectives.
- Possibilities are realized through the hard work of repeated, incremental, step-by-step practice.

APPLYING THE CONCEPTS TO YOUR LIFE

1. What possibilities do I believe in?
2. How well do I focus on the possibilities I believe in?
3. What are three actions I can take to be more effective in pursuing these possibilities?
4. Who can help me be accountable for taking these steps?
5. What, if anything, is holding me back from achieving these possibilities?
6. What are some mental barriers that may be preventing me from making progress?

7. What are the limiting ideas and behaviors that may be sabotaging my progress?

8. How do others' expectations of me affect my results?

9. What kind of self-talk am I using – is it positively or negatively reinforcing?

10. Complete the following statements, creating positive – perhaps new – language you can use to replace old limiting thoughts:

I am ...   I am working toward ...

I can ...   I am creating ...

I do ...

Note how important it is to keep your language in the present tense. Avoid future-based language like "I will..." to create the most effective affirmations.

For worksheets and additional exercises geared at living possibilities, visit FindFulfill-Flourish.com; then click on Book & Tools.

Chapter 9

Life Leadership: The First Person You Must Lead Is Yourself

Initiating the process

Making it happen for yourself and others

Creating a new future

Life Leadership from Scratch: Tim Lewis and the Compton Little League

Imagine an adolescent boy growing up with a single mom in a tough, inner city neighborhood. Sensing that he was born into a life of violence, he's now under pressure to join a gang and is resigned to the fact that selling drugs will be a part of his future. That's simply the way many young people earn money in Compton, California.

On the other hand, he is intrigued by the Little League diamond he walks past every day. He watches the fun and camaraderie shared by the boys who play, and is invited to join a game by coach Tim Lewis. Tim becomes a different kind of role model for him, and the father figure he never had. The boy learns that Tim also led a hardscrabble life, and has lifted himself up from homelessness and addiction to the role of a community leader. He was down, and learned how to rise up. "He can relate to me," the boy thinks, "to who I am and the struggles I deal with every day."

This is precisely the type of challenge Tim faces frequently as he introduces kids from this drug- and gang-riddled Los Angeles suburb to Little League baseball. He motivates them to participate and gives them a positive alternative to gang life.

* * *

Tim Lewis was 52, homeless, and living out of his 1993 Toyota Camry. He slept and ate in his car, parked on a street near Sibrie Park in Compton, California. Forty years earlier, Tim had played Little League Baseball in this very park. Back then, it was called El Segundo Park. Some of the guys he played with went on to become Major Leaguers, including Lonnie Smith, Reggie Smith, and Roy White. Most were African American and Latino. Little League ended at the park in 1979, as the neighborhood went the way of many inner city communities, becoming a haven for crime, gang violence, and drug dealing. Just about anyone who has heard of Compton knows of its reputation as a tough neighborhood.

Tim followed in the footsteps of many from Compton. He became an alcoholic and drug addict and got caught up in crime. His choices ruined his dreams of going to college on a band scholarship, severed his relationships with several women he loved, and destroyed his relationships with his children. In essence, he sabotaged any hopes he might have had of building the life he desired. Even after finding enough strength to get himself into rehab, he relapsed a number of times, creating a life that amounted to little more than a despaired series of aimless wanderings.

Through it all, one thing stayed with Tim: he remembered the local baseball field where he played Little League, and that some of his teammates had made it to the Majors. He recalled how, in his youth, the field was well maintained with a functional scoreboard. Over the years, the scoreboard disappeared and the field deteriorated from neglect, becoming pocked with holes. As the neighborhood youth were seduced into lives of gang violence and crime, not even the town's baseball field was spared.

For Tim, though, the park was still a bit of a retreat. It was where he went to think, stretch, breathe, and remember how things used to be. Living on the street, he saw firsthand what was happening to the kids and to his hometown.

"You can't lead anyone else further than you have gone yourself."
— Gene Mauch

He thought about how the negative changes had affected him and his life. As he thought about his skills, his experiences growing up in Compton, and his love of baseball, an idea began to materialize for Tim. He began to see possibilities – and believe in them. And when Tim had the opportunity to present his idea, he took the initiative. Tim met Compton's mayor, Eric Perrodin, at a bicycle fair and explained that he wanted to give back to the community. He described his desire to resurrect Little League Baseball and help steer the neighborhood kids away from a life he knew led nowhere. It was an extraordinary goal, especially for someone whose life had been chock-full of struggle and dismay.

Mayor Perrodin listened, and Tim was on his way. His next step was to engage others. He met with James Moore, a paramedic with the Compton Fire Department, who contacted Little League headquarters to acquire a charter. James became the League's president, and Tim worked on recruiting players. Together, they sought donations to get things started. Their successes included a $10,000 contribution from Torii Hunter, an All Star center fielder for the Los Angeles Angels. The money they raised paid for the charter, uniforms, equipment, and advertising. This seed money also ensured that parents would not have to pay registration fees.

Tim is now comanager of the Compton Braves, part of the Little League he restored, which has grown to include several teams. He is a role model for his players and others in Compton. He coaches, encourages, and has even become a father figure to some. He is an inspiration. Tim teaches about second chances – and offers them. He demonstrates the importance of giving your best, even when losing, and how to learn from losses and rebound from setbacks. As Tim turned around these neighborhood kids, giving them an alternative to gangs and crime by reviving the Compton Little League, he turned his own life around. He found his passion, and through his work, blessings returned to him.

Today, Tim plans to go back to school to requalify to become a surgical technician, a field he worked in long ago, before walking away from it and several other jobs. Now he has a new direction for his life, and has discovered what is fulfilling and meaningful for him. It all started with a desire to create a better future, coupled with an act of leadership. Tim Lewis is a perfect example of life leadership.

A story about Tim Lewis, "Stepping Up to the Plate in Compton," by Ben Bolch, appeared in the Los Angeles Times *on May 27, 2009. Mr. Lewis also was profiled on the August 18, 2009 edition of HBO's* Real Sports *with Bryant Gumbel.*

The Concept of Life Leadership

Just as Tim Lewis found the key to unlocking his own life by taking the lead to help others, we can all do the same. The only thing it requires is self-leadership.

Most of us want to make the most of our lives, and each individual goes about this in his or her own unique way. Yet there are certain ingredients required if we wish to achieve this goal.

> Life leadership refers to the ability to take initiative and guide your life and activities toward achieving your vision, in the process of finding personal fulfillment and meaning. It involves transforming your vision and purpose into reality.

So far, we have discussed the "Cycle of Inspiration and Personal Fulfillment" and the importance of values, vision, action, spirituality, relationships, engaging others, and focusing on possibilities. Another critical element is life leadership.

Leadership has been defined many ways. Life leadership refers to the ability to take the initiative to guide your life and activities toward achieving your vision, finding personal fulfillment and meaning in the process. It involves transforming your vision and purpose into reality.

Rosamund Zander, leadership coach and coauthor with Benjamin Zander of *The Art of Possibility*, speaks of leadership in a similar vein. She makes the point, "[W]hen leadership is defined not as a position you hold, but as a way of being, you discover that you can lead from wherever you are." You can lead your life – and others, if you choose – from any point, no matter where that may be. Leading your own life constructively establishes a foundation for leading others, and positions you as a model for them to emulate.

Leading your life congruently involves modeling the life and world you envision by living according to your values. Life leadership is about guiding yourself to new places in the future and creating something valuable. Life leadership is about realizing possibilities.

Contrast the concept of life leadership with "managing." People sometimes ask, "How are you managing?" This generally refers to coping – how you are getting by. Managing is most often present oriented. It focuses on how you are conducting and arranging your life in this moment, or how you might be getting through a challenging time or situation. It is usually about implementing and maintaining what is.

If you want what you have right now, then keep doing what you have been doing – continue managing as you have been. If you are seeking a better, more fulfilling, and meaningful life, you must lead yourself there. That involves vision, initiative, action, positive focus, engaging others, and adherence to your personal values.

Here is our definition of life leadership:

> **Generating and sustaining momentum to pursue a vision and purpose, achieve goals, create opportunities, and develop and pursue new arenas of achievement by consistently demonstrating personal values, taking proactive responsibility, and engaging and inspiring others.**

A "new arena of achievement" is a fresh purpose-focused endeavor that will move you closer to your vision. "Proactive responsibility" involves taking the initiative and accepting accountability for achieving your dream; in other words – your vision and the accomplishments that lead to it.

Our definition of life leadership may seem complex. You may think that demonstrating it would be a monumental task. In reality, it is relatively simple and straightforward. Let's look at how Tim Lewis' initiative to resurrect Little League baseball in Compton, California fits the definition.

• **Pursue a vision and purpose**	*Tim pursued his vision of restoring Little League Baseball and using it as an attractive means to engage local youth and draw them away from gangs, drugs, and violence.*
• **Achieve goals**	*He achieved a series of goals to make this happen – from first getting the mayor's support and then raising money to recruit players.*
• **Create opportunities**	*The Little League he revived created opportunities and new options for disadvantaged youth and their parents.*
• **Develop and pursue new arenas of achievement**	*Tim brought into existence the Compton teams that were the cornerstone of his vision and purpose.*

- **Consistently demonstrate personal values**

  Tim became a role model for the youth of his community, daily living and teaching values such as accountability, community, kindness, compassion, fairness, fun, joy, humility and teamwork.

- **Take proactive responsibility**

  He took initiative to make it happen. Without his action, nothing would have occurred.

- **Engage and inspire others**

  The people he engaged and inspired included community professionals and leaders, parents, and the kids – as well as all those from a greater distance, who were inspired by his example.

Tim Lewis is a living example of life leadership in action. He knew what was possible from his own experience and was inspired. He naturally demonstrated life leadership in the course of developing his purpose-enhanced life and pursuing his vision. His accomplishment was not achieved through magic. It required work, determination, and action to achieve great possibilities. Tim's passion for helping youth and his love of baseball drove his actions. In the process, he led his own life and the life of his community to new and better places.

Here is another example of life leadership. Twelve-year-old Talia was required to fulfill a community service project for school. She had to choose an area of service where she would devote thirteen hours of her time. She discovered an organization called Parenthesis, a nonprofit whose goal is to strengthen family bonds and facilitate the development of parents and young children. One of its programs is devoted to single-parent families. Each Tuesday, parents bring their infants and toddlers to the center for education. While the parents are in class, Talia, an assistant to a childcare professional, tends their children. Although Talia has completed her thirteen hours of community service, she was so excited by the work that she continues to volunteer. The work has become part of her self-definition, and she now makes her family, social, and school plans around this commitment.

Life leadership has three aspects:

1. Knowing who you are and having the strength of character to be that person.
2. Determining where you wish to lead yourself.
3. Deciding whether you want to move beyond self-

leadership to lead others.

The first part of leading your life is knowing who you are and having the strength of character to be that person. Strength of character is reflected in your track record for courageously living your values, even under adverse conditions, when pressure or expedience might tempt you to pursue a path that compromises your values and beliefs. You reflect your identity and character by how congruent your stated values are with your actions.

Staying true to yourself requires three ingredients: self-trust, integrity, and intent. Self-trust means being solid in your decisions and not second-guessing yourself. Integrity means living your values and beliefs – being consistent with who you say you are. Intent refers to your motives. Whose best interests do you have in mind? Who or what drives your actions? Do you have ulterior motives or hidden agendas? Is your focus the personal or short-term advantage for a few or the long-term benefit for many? Ultimately, you are responsible for yourself, both today and as you continue on your LifePath.

The second part of personal leadership is determining where you wish to lead yourself. It is leadership connecting with purpose and vision. Your purpose and vision may grow and evolve over time. They may change significantly over the course of your life as you acquire further knowledge, face challenges, experience various levels of success, and adapt to the changing world around you. Nonetheless, you need to begin with your personal North Star.

Christopher Columbus' purpose for his first voyage across the Atlantic Ocean was to discover a sea route to India. He did not know there was a "New World" to be discovered. He did not know what he did not know, just like most of us when we begin our own voyages of discovery. Columbus took a huge risk that was based on his strong conviction. With three Spanish ships and a combined crew of forty men, he pursued his passion despite incredible odds. He was driven by the challenge, as well as by the potential wealth his voyage might generate for Spain and himself. Columbus' motives for taking this gamble included a complex mix of pursuing a greater good for the Spanish royalty, personal fame for discovering a sea route to a distant continent that could benefit many, and strong financial self-interest. The latter two probably represented his concept of personal fulfillment – although he likely would not have labeled it as such.

There is nothing inherently wrong with pursuing self-interest. We all do it. It is a prime motivator, and plenty of good can result from it. As we discussed in Chapter 1, "The Personal Journey to *Find Fulfill Flourish*," purpose and self-interest are intertwined. Innovation and applied ingenuity depend on them. In the past, these have led to the invention and availability of innumerable modern conveniences, many of which are now considered necessities. The key is to balance self-interest and personal ambition with larger benefits for causes beyond ourselves.

Pursuit of pure self-interest may work for a while. In most cases, however, it eventually catches up with us and may backfire in a painful way. Individuals who put their own self-interest first and only superficially combine it with the intention of producing a greater good are often described as greedy, selfish, corrupt, or untrustworthy. In some cases, approaches based on self-interest alone can lead to huge ethical lapses and significant breaches of trust. We need look no further than fallen leaders in business, labor unions, politics, government, and even the nonprofit sector to see examples. Leaders who put personal self-interest first have been convicted of serious offenses and received lengthy prison sentences.

Columbus did not know that the islands he sailed to, more than 4,000 miles from Spain, were actually close to a continent unknown to Europeans at the time. Few of us are so fortunate to follow a hunch, mistakenly land in an unknown place, and succeed beyond our expectations. Yet that is the risk and excitement of leading oneself – and possibly others – into the unknown. We never really know what we will find or learn when we first set off in pursuit of a passion, set forth on a journey, or strive to achieve our vision for the future. It takes a leader to make that happen. Life leadership is a process of exploration and discovery. We each have an inner leader inside of us, even if the only person we choose to lead is ourselves.

The third part of life leadership is deciding whether you want to move beyond the bounds of self leadership to lead others in a purpose-driven enterprise. You can achieve significant and meaningful accomplishments that are deeply gratifying by containing your passion to your own personal endeavors. And quite possibly, your example and good works will inspire others. You may also choose to lead others. In enlisting others in your purpose and leading them, you can expand your reach and influence, widening the scope of your purpose and vision. By engaging and leading others, you can achieve possibilities far beyond what one person can accomplish alone; as a cohesive team, you can have a much greater impact. You can accomplish by spearheading an organization, as an endeavor within a larger organization, or as a joint venture with another leader or team of visionaries.

By leading others, one individual can create community, societal, or global impact through the arts, public speaking, a website, social media, advocacy, volunteer activities, and other actions. Conversely, one can have quite a visible position with community, societal, or global responsibilities and still have little impact.

Life Leadership Principles

Below are five overarching personal leadership principles that, when embraced and integrated into how you live and lead your life, can generate tremendous good. These principles recapitulate many concepts we have explored so far, so you can view them as a whole. They also reflect the interconnected nature of the Eight Dynamics in the LifePath model.

1. Define yourself by what you are, your passion, and what you want to be.
2. Invest in relationships and develop others.
3. Put the best interests of your goals and the people involved in achieving them above your own.
4. Emulate your vision.
5. Believe the "impossible" is possible.

For a deeper exploration of these five leadership principles, please visit FindFulfillFlourish.com. Go to the Book & Tools tab and click on Additional Application Exercises.

* * *

Though he didn't start out as one, Tim Lewis became a leader. He built his passion and purpose from a life of despair. When he started, he had nothing but his car, a few possessions, and his life. He had failed at many things. He did have heart, however, and believed that with a little help he could make a big difference. He shared his inspiration and inspired others with his vision of a better world for the youth in his neighborhood. He has since rejuvenated many lives that might otherwise have followed a path similar to his own destructive journey.

It matters not where your starting point is, nor does it matter how much money or status you have, how old you are, or whether you have a job or a track record. What matters is transforming your inspiration into a clear purpose, taking initiative, and supporting your idea with action and your own brand of leadership – starting with yourself.

NAVIGATIONAL POINTS

- The key to unlocking your own life is through engaging with others.
- Life leadership is about taking initiative and steering your life and your actions to achieve your vision and purpose.
- Life leadership requires a future-oriented mindset.
- Pursue new arenas of achievement to advance toward your vision.
- Life leadership involves three parts:
  1. Demonstrating strength of character by consistently exhibiting the values you claim to embrace.
  2. Determining where you want to go, taking initiative, and persistently pursuing your goals.
  3. Deciding whether to move beyond self leadership to lead others, and if so, engaging them.

APPLYING THE CONCEPTS TO YOUR LIFE

1. Am I presently pursuing a purpose? If so, how passionately am I pursuing it?
2. What goal do I have for improving my life leadership?
3. What are three actions I can take to become a more effective leader of myself and/or others?
4. What are some of the initiatives I'd like to pursue?
5. What are some new areas of achievement I can develop?
6. What kind of future do I want to create?
7. What are the next steps I must take to create that future?

For worksheets and additional exercises on Life Leadership, visit FindFulfillFlourish. com and click on Book & Tools.

Chapter 10

Choices: Change Your Choices, Change Your Life

Considering alternatives

Choosing who you want to be

Modeling your values

Life-Transforming Choices:
Yosef Garcia and the Association of Crypto-Jews of the Americas

Tears stream down Pablo Garcia Perez's face as he speaks Spanish and broken English. Two brothers, Samuel and Saul Saldana, also are overcome by the significance of this moment, as are ten other Hispanic worshipers. All have just completed a family journey spanning five hundred years and more than twenty-five generations, since Jews were expelled en masse from Spain and Portugal. These men and women's ancestors fled the Iberian Peninsula to Latin America in search of religious freedom, but found only continued suppression. Many practiced their faith secretly; some converted to Catholicism; still others merely pretended to do so. But regardless of their choice, their connection to Judaism became thinner and thinner over the centuries.

Eventually, the connection all but vanished – except for a few rituals that were passed down, such as lighting candles on Friday evenings, usually in the basement or some other hidden area, and covering mirrors when a family member died. However, five hundred years later, very few of the descendents had any idea why they, their parents, or their grandparents performed these rituals – other than their being very long-standing family customs. The vast majority were unaware of their Jewish lineage, although all sensed that they and their heritage were somehow different from the overwhelmingly Christian or Catholic culture in which they lived. The few who did know of their Jewish ancestry were told secretly by a parent or grandparent, or they stumbled upon the information accidently.

Yosef Garcia was one of these displaced descendants. Yet today, he is the rabbi leading the ceremony in which these twelve men and women officially return to Judaism. Yosef has been teaching, counseling, and coaching these individuals for the past thirty months, helping them rediscover and live the faith and heritage of their ancestors and teaching them to raise their children as Jews. A rabbi is on call nights and weekends. Furthermore, it is a job for which he receives little or no compensation, since his congregants have low-paying jobs and are economically disadvantaged. Nonetheless, this is the work and the purpose to which Rabbi Garcia has dedicated his life.

* * *

Yosef's parents met when his father, a soldier in the U.S. Army, was stationed in the Panama Canal Zone. His mother was Panamanian and became a naturalized U.S. citizen. Yosef was born in Oklahoma while his father was stationed stateside. When her husband was deployed overseas for an extended period, Yosef's mother chose to move herself and her son to Panama, rather than move with the military.

In Panama, Yosef was raised as a good Catholic, active in the church and serving as an altar boy. Finding the priests had no satisfying answers to his inquiries about God and Catholicism, he eventually stopped attending church altogether. Yosef remembers sensing that something was missing and the feeling that his whole life was a haze. His spiritual curiosity continued.

As a young adult, Yosef returned to the United States, settling in Seattle.

Now married, he sought to reconnect with God. It was at this time that Yosef chose to go back and explore his sacred texts. Realizing he knew little about the Bible, he began to read it closely and to discuss it with others. He thought the opinions and interpretations of others might help shed light and lift his haze, but this process only led to more questions. In his desire to gain the truest understanding possible, Yosef made another choice that permanently altered the direction of his LifePath. Yosef chose to study Hebrew, thinking that reading the work in its original language might sate his thirst for understanding.

A while later, at the age of thirty-two, Yosef attended his brother's wedding in Florida. He was catching up with his great uncle, Chi Chi, when he mentioned his choice to study Hebrew. Chi Chi shocked Yosef by telling him that, based on his lineage, Yosef was Jewish. Chi Chi revealed that his own Hebrew name was Chaim, and that he was a practicing Jew.

Yosef was stunned, asking, "Why has no one told me?" Chi Chi replied, "The only family members who know are those who asked." Yosef immediately sought out his mother and, already knowing the answer, asked if she knew that they were Jewish; she told him that she knew.

Like a detective, Yosef put together various clues from his past, bit by bit. He remembered watching his grandmother lighting candles on Friday night and saying blessings in an unfamiliar language he now realized was Hebrew. She had been bringing in the Sabbath day, a custom she learned from her grandmother. He recalled that when his aunt died, his mother covered the mirrors in their home, a common Jewish practice meant to shift the focus away from oneself and one's looks during the grieving process. Yosef began to recognize that the various practices he once thought simply old family customs were actually Judaic laws and rituals.

All of this information, combined with his persistent spiritual yearning, led Yosef to his next choice: he return to Judaism. Although some mainstream rabbis denied his Jewish lineage, insisting he was Catholic, he nevertheless continued his studies of Judaism and Hebrew. During this process, Yosef met Rabbi Joshua Stampfer, of Congregation Neveh Shalom in Portland, Oregon, one of the founders of the Society for Crypto Judaic Studies. Crypto Jews are people of Judaic lineage who practice Judaism privately to avoid detection and persecution while maintaining the pretense of practicing another faith, or who have maintained some Jewish rituals while outwardly affiliating with another religion.

Yosef returned to Panama and continued studying Judaism under the guidance of Rabbi Levi. Rabbi Levi got to know him well and told Yosef that he would make a great rabbi, suggesting that in doing so, Yosef could help many others return to Judaism. This suggestion caused Yosef to reflect on the extensive study and life-long commitment such an undertaking would entail, and he wondered whether it was the right path for him. After officially completing his own return to Judaism, Yosef made the commitment.

Moving back to the United States, Yosef began his rabbinic studies with Rabbi Zalman Schachter Shalomi. He was ordained in 2004 at the age of forty-nine. He was then invited to work with Rabbi Stampfer, a natural choice for him. Together, they have helped several hundred Crypto Jews return to Judaism. The process takes two years, educating students in Jewish history and rituals, holidays, prayer, and the laws of keeping kosher. The seekers must also learn the Hebrew language.

Yosef has met few individuals who are aware of the descendents of Jews who migrated from Spain or Portugal as a result of their expulsions from those countries, or of their unique culture. Scant details are known of the history of these Jews once they made their way to South or Central America. It is a missing chapter in most texts on the Diaspora, yet it is somewhat analogous to the history of Jews who went underground during the Holocaust. Sephardic Jews (those from Spain or nearby Mediterranean countries) were exiled from Spain as a result of the Inquisitions that began in 1492 and remained underground for centuries, while their more modern counterparts during the Nazi reign hid throughout Europe for a number of years. Both were fearful of persecution or mistreatment by their surrounding cultures. The most startling thing about the Crypto Jews is their immense numbers.

Yosef, now Rabbi Garcia, was inspired to bring the Crypto Jewish experience to light and to help as many descendants of Spanish and Portuguese Jews as he could return to Judaism. He joined the Society for Judaic Studies and formed The Association of Crypto Jews of the Americas with Rabbi Stampfer. Early in his rabbinic career, Rabbi Garcia helped largely middle-class Crypto Jews in Portland, Oregon return to Judaism. When he learned of the great need of very poor Crypto Jews in the American Southwest, he moved with his wife, Yvonne, to the Phoenix area. There he founded Avde Torah Hayah, the first synagogue dedicated to serving this specialized Sephardic community and helping Crypto Jews return to the faith of their ancestors.

Today, Rabbi Garcia works throughout the Southwest, from California to Texas, as well as in parts of Mexico, reaching out to help his fellow Sephardic Crypto Jews. He also engages via regular web conferences with communities in Brazil, Peru, Costa Rica, Puerto Rico, Montreal, and even Germany, to offer spiritual leaders in those countries tools to help Crypto Jews make their return.

When asked why the return is so important to him, Yosef pauses. He dodges the question. But as he is asked again, he reflects. He says initially, "I want people to have the option to say 'No' to Judaism," because it is safe to assume that many

Crypto Jews are satisfied with the religious identities they have adopted over the centuries. But Yosef speaks again of the haze he experienced, as if there is something inside Crypto Jews that stirs a feeling of incongruence, an ambiguous sense that they are out of alignment. "I want them to remember God. What gives me great joy and what motivates me to get up early before my day job and to go to bed late every night is helping them find answers to their questions about

> "We find ourselves walking through life in a haze becasue we are not really sure if we are on the right path. I help people answer the questions of 'Who am I?' and 'What am I doing here?'"

God. We find ourselves walking through life in a haze because we are not really sure if we are on the right path. I help them answer the questions of 'Who am I?' 'What am I doing here?' and 'Why am I here?' I want to let them know that God has not left them behind. Because you're Jewish, you are pushed by God to come back," says Yosef. "I want them to have that choice."

An eighty-five-year-old man in a wheelchair approaches Rabbi Garcia and says, "You know, rabbi, I have been waiting my whole life for someone to tell me I am Jewish and to make me feel welcome in the Jewish community." Moments like this are the essence of why he does this work.

Rabbi Garcia's face lights up when he helps others journey back to Judaism. Much of what was lost to these families during their centuries in the "wilderness" is now being found and restored. Seeing that happen, one individual or family at a time, is immensely gratifying and fulfilling for Yosef. Equally profound is watching the children of these returned Jews grow up in the Jewish faith. The children attending the Avde Torah Hayah religious school fully identify as Jews, not as Crypto Jews. This generation is the future of a renewed and thriving Hispanic Sephardic Jewish community.

Rabbi Garcia's journey is still in its early stages, but he has a big vision. He believes millions of Hispanic descendents of Jews expelled from the Iberian Peninsula are living in the Americas. One estimate puts the number as high as thirty-two million. Rabbi Garcia knows he has reached a very small percentage, far less than even the tip of the iceberg. His vision is that all those who yearn to return to Judaism be able to, and that future generations be assimilated into the mainstream Jewish community while retaining the Hispanic cultural characteristics that make them unique.

Achieving his vision is presently limited by his meager resources. Today, most of the funding for his congregation comes out of his own pocket, from his earnings as a telecommunications engineer. He aims to generate support from the broader Jewish community, believing this cause is an important element in the future of the greater Jewish community. Yosef has chosen to add two components to his work: the education of the mainstream Jewish community about Crypto Jews and fundraising to support their return. At a time when many American Jews take their faith for granted, are unaffiliated, or have drifted away from their heritage, these Crypto Jews are passionate about rediscovering and living their faith. It has great meaning and significance for them.

"Sometimes I cry and get discouraged because I find myself looking around, thinking, 'I'm out here all by myself. Did I make the right decision?'" Rabbi Garcia knows of several others like him who have been inspired to help Crypto Jews return to Judaism. They are studying, but it will be another four to five years before these new leaders will be ready to help him. "Then I get a phone call from somebody saying, 'Rabbi, you changed my life, and I can't thank you enough.' And I know it's worth it. I have personally helped hundreds of people reconnect to Judaism, but to have helped just that one individual make it back into the Jewish community would have been worth it."

Beginning in his early adulthood, Rabbi Yosef Garcia made profound choices in his life that significantly affected his LifePath. He continues to make those choices today as he expands his work, reaching more Crypto Jews with each passing month, and as he works to engage and educate the larger Jewish community of which they are a part. Through his work, each day he helps others make profound choices of their own.

Find more information about the Association of Crypto-Jews of the Americas at cryptojew.org.

Our Identity and Our Choices

Our choices define who we are and the level of fulfillment we ultimately achieve. Each of us is responsible for our own results. Likewise, we are responsible for the kind of person we choose to be. Although our culture, government, environment, and socio-economic conditions play a role, it is ultimately the innumerable choices we make that shape and define us as unique individuals. These choices determine how meaningful our lives become to both ourselves and others.

Finding your purpose, what is meaningful and fulfilling to you, usually is not a straight path. More than likely, you will experience twists, turns, false starts, wrong turns, detours, and setbacks.

You will probably get lost from time to time, just like Yosef did. You may decide to retrace your steps so you can return to familiar ground and then take another path, or you may stop to get your bearings and make mid-course corrections to get back on track. Knowing your life purpose and where you want to go will help you become more centered in making these decisions.

> Choices become real when they are accompaniend by actions. Otherwise, they are not really choices. Without actions to support our choices, we appear to be inauthentic.

In Chapter 4, "Values: You Are What You Value," we discussed that HOW we live our lives (our values), WHAT we are about (our purpose), and WHERE we take ourselves (our vision and aspirations) are all connected. We cannot achieve our vision or realize our purpose by living counter to what we proclaim our values to be. Because the vitality of our purpose and vision depends on the choices we make and how we model the values we advocate, we must consistently demonstrate our commitment to this purpose and vision as we work to create the life of our dreams. The decision to demonstrate this commitment is perhaps the most essential choice we make related to finding the fulfillment we seek.

Life is full of choices. In fact, every day is full of choices, ranging from big, life-changing decisions, like the ones made by Yosef Garcia, to moment-to-moment decisions. Our choices, in large part, characterize us as individuals and shape the perceptions others form about us. Choices and actions are intertwined. First we choose, and then our actions confirm and implement the choice – demonstrating our commitment. Choices become real when they are accompanied by actions. Otherwise, they cannot truly be considered choices. Without actions that support our choices, we appear inauthentic, possibly even seeming to choose the opposite of what we claim. The actions that follow our choices influence our future, defining our purpose, direction, and the possibilities we will achieve. Our collective choices have a profound impact on our sense of fulfillment, how we feel about ourselves, and how others see us.

LifePath Choices

We make all kinds of choices in life: choices about relationships; choices about education; choices about career; choices about where to live; choices about long-term commitments. We also make choices about our purpose in life, how we wish to live, and the direction in which we want to steer ourselves – sometimes with great awareness and intention, and sometimes almost accidentally.

These macro choices may be made in an instant or over an extended period of contemplation. The choices Yosef made about his faith and his LifePath evolved over time, as a consequence of extensive study, deep thought, emotional connection, and a yearning for a greater mission in life. His choices transformed his life and his life purpose.

These big choices influence our LifePath in significant ways. They alter or confirm our current path, often carrying us toward a bold new future. Whether they change our course by one degree or many degrees, any new path will lead to the discovery of new territory, allowing us to explore new ways of impacting the world and creating opportunities for further personal growth and fulfillment.

While macro choices tend to have long-term significance, the micro – or seemingly small – choices we make every day also shape our future. Micro choices are often related to how we do things, while macro choices more often are about where we are going and what we actually accomplish. Together, they form the tapestry of our identities and lives, although it can be easier to see the impact of the macro choices on our lives and more difficult to appreciate the impact of our micro choices. The micro choices are, nevertheless, profound in their impact.

Connie, for example, recently separated from her husband. In her early sixties, she finds herself searching for a new sense of identity and stability, because everything she has known for the past forty years has suddenly turned topsy-turvy. Connie isn't thinking about starting a big volunteer project or heading a committee right now, but she knows she finds value and identity in service, so she is always on the lookout for ways to contribute. On Monday mornings, she rises early and prepares food and coffee for her local congregation's prayer service. She regularly visits the sick and the grieving. She asks what her friends and community members need, and ever alert for an individual or a situation that might need her help. Her presence is a true gift to her community. Even while Connie is dealing with her own personal struggles, she is doing the work of a heartisan on a regular basis. Her micro choices bring her fulfillment at an unstable moment in her life, while allowing her to make a difference in others' lives.

Our Moods

From the moment we get up in the morning, we begin to set our tone for the day. We can either consciously decide what our mood will be, choosing to be happy, optimistic, or joyful, or we can simply allow the mood we awake with to carry the day, even if it's crabby and dour. Steve Lundon, in his business bestseller, *Fish*, describes the remarkable attitude overhaul of the staff at Pike Place Fish Market in Seattle. Fighting for greater market share in a competitive retail business, the owners chose to differentiate their business by making shopping for fish fun. Achieving that objective required creating entirely new ways for the employees to present themselves, sell fresh fish, and interact with customers. It meant everyone had to choose, every day, to have fun and create fun. To do so, employees had to choose to be joyful, no matter how they felt when they rolled out of bed or showed up for work.

The choice to focus on employee behavior became a way of business that attracted throngs of customers to Pike who had never paid much attention to the store before, and sales skyrocketed. In the process, the decision to make buying fish a fun, joyful experience brightened the days of everyone around them – from customers to coworkers. It made the entire workday exciting and enjoyable. Such a simple choice gave greater purpose and meaning to the seemingly mundane process of buying and selling fish. In addition to vending a food staple, Pike creates happiness and makes each customer's day every day.

How can you apply this lesson to your work and life? What choices can you make that are appropriate to your work or vision that might ultimately increase your success while enhancing the lives of others? We can see through the example of Pike Place Fish Market that something as simple as choosing to be in a good mood each day can have a huge impact, much greater than you might imagine – and will likely contribute to your living a more satisfying life.

Think about the people you are drawn to and enjoy being around. Think about those you know who reliably get things done and whom others freely follow. Most of us prefer to surround ourselves with people who bring joy and stimulation to our lives. The interesting thing is that these people often are involved in something substantive and meaningful. Their commitment and focus on the greater good lead us to perceive them as fun, interesting, and enjoyable.

Just as uplifting emotions like joy and happiness can facilitate our search for meaning and purpose, unpleasant emotions such as anger, hostility, and resentment can become barriers. These emotions tend to drive people away. They also can affect our efficiency and focus. While negative emotions may result from aggravating or unpredictable circumstances, we always have the ability to choose how we respond. The key is to notice ourselves beginning to react negatively to a situation, and catch it before it goes too far. Through practice, we can learn to maintain our peace and balance, rather than allowing situations to affect our dispositions. We always have a choice.

INNER QUEST
Where are some new, invigorating choices you'd like to make?

OUTER QUEST
How will your new choices support who you want to be for others, as well as the impact you want to make?

You may be thinking, "Being positive or adjusting my outlook is just not something I can do. I am who I am, I've always been this way, and that's it." You may feel we are suggesting that you behave as someone you are not. This is not our intention. While we recognize that each person is unique and that we all have propensities to act in certain ways, every single one of us can make improvements. Each of us can find a way to become the best person we can be.

Are You in a Rut?

If you find yourself stuck in a negative spiral, it's important that you find a way to shift your mental and emotional states. The employees at Pike Place Fish Market were able to do so – even those who were at first reluctant or non-believers. A proven behavioral principle is that attitude change follows behavioral change, not the other way around, as is commonly asserted.

While this may seem counterintuitive, we suggest you begin by consciously making choices about your moods and the attitudes you project, and then observe the impact for yourself. The following steps may help:

- Choose a behavior you would like to exemplify during your day (happy, optimistic, friendly, etc.) and set it as your compass. We find the best time to do this is first thing in the morning.
- Remind yourself of your choice throughout the day.
- Acknowledge yourself at day's end, even if you only experienced modest success.

Remember, learning to demonstrate a new attitude is just like learning anything else in life: it takes sustained effort and continued practice. Implement these steps for just for a week or two, and observe the results in your life and in the lives of others you touch. The benefits may become apparent in as little as a matter of days. You might then discover you no longer need to make daily or moment-to-moment decisions about your mood because the new choices have simply become instinctive. The Pike employees didn't make their shift overnight, but once they made it, everything changed.

Ethics and Values

Ethical choices come in all shapes and sizes. Ethical dilemmas often present a trade-off between doing the right thing versus seeking temporary advantages. Other times, they amount to potential long-term advantages via ill-gotten gains. Life is full of temptations, some of which may not be in our best interest. These choices may prove to be profound dilemmas that are difficult to discern. Such decisions can push our values and test our character. Another type of dilemma occurs when two or more values conflict with each other. In such situations, we must weigh the values and the effect of selecting one choice over the other. We can see this demonstrated by Betty's story.

Ruth's aging mother, Betty, was quite ill and frail. Ruth spent a great deal of time with Betty, as they lived near each other in San Diego. Ruth's sister, Jeanette, lived in Baltimore and would phone Betty every other day. The doctor had been warning the daughter for months about causing Betty any undue stress, as doing so might significantly affect her health for the worse.

Ruth was on her way to visit Betty when the phone rang. It was Jeanette, frantic with fear. Her breast lumps had been diagnosed as cancer, and she needed a double mastectomy. The two commiserated for a while until the question arose, "What do we tell mom?" Ruth and Jeanette had always maintained an open, honest relationship with their mother, and Ruth knew her mother would want to know about her sister's condition, but given the doctor's strong caution, she wasn't sure what to do.

Likewise, Jeanette was feeling vulnerable and very much wanted her mother's support, but was also sensitive to her mom's needs.

Should they tell their mother about Jeanette's cancer or not? Betty was very perceptive and would notice if Ruth seemed distracted. She would also hear the tension in Jeanette's voice on the phone or notice if she missed calling, even for a few days while she had surgery and was recovering. Betty would wonder and ask what was going on. Should the sisters say nothing or construct a cover-up story? They had to weigh their desire for their mother's support against what was best for her.

There is no right or wrong answer in this story. Each of us must weigh the issues and makes the choices we think are best in a given situation, based on who we are and the complexity of the issues involved.

The stories of Yosef Garcia, Pike Place Fish Market, and Ruth, Jeanette and Betty demonstrate clearly that choices affect our lives in many different arenas. They affect our LifePath, our success in business, our relationships, our daily outlook, even our self-esteem. They affect the way others see us and the kinds of people we draw to ourselves. Positive choices tend to attract positive people; negative choices bring negative people. The power of our choices cannot be underscored enough, because they affect every part of our lives. Below are few areas that exemplify just how important our choices are.

Relationships

The relationships we develop and maintain are among our most precious assets and are crucial to finding meaning and personal fulfillment. They can be a source of both the greatest joys we have in life and the greatest hurt. Most accomplishments are realized with and through others. Yet relationships can unravel, and their demise can be immensely painful.

Solving Problems versus Being Right

Many people have a strong need to be right. We may see it in conversations with family, friends, and coworkers. It shows up in organizational meetings, in political discussions, and in many other situations. The focus on proving our point – and being right – is often mutually exclusive from truly listening to others, considering the merits of their perspectives, honestly entertaining other possibilities, or critically and objectively examining our own positions. Sometimes in our effort to be right, we deny facts or truths apparent to others; we also selectively use information that supports our preferred position or promotes a hidden agenda.

Business

We need only look at the Pike Place Fish Market to see how powerful the effect of one simple choice can be. The way we treat our coworkers, employees, and clients has a profound effect on them. Choosing to be kind, patient, warm, and joyful will set an inviting tone for our business endeavors. Making the choice to focus on results at the expense of people may bring a different kind of outcome, perhaps with a result opposite the one you desire. How we treat people directly affects their desire to continue doing business with us.

Daily Choices and Life Impact

Every moment, we face choices. We can, in any given situation, decide to move forward or back, side to side, or even at an angle. We can jump or sit. Every question we face, every single circumstance we encounter, offers myriad ways for us to respond.

Each day at work, we choose how to start our day and which tasks to tackle first. Do we begin with the true priorities, or the items we most enjoy? Do we adhere rigidly to a routine, or flex to accommodate changing circumstances? Like the employees at Pike Place Fish Market, we can choose our demeanor -- to be bright, perky, happy, positive, cooperative, open-minded and receptive, or to be rigid, cold, mean-spirited, unwilling, depressed, negative, stubborn, and all-knowing. In certain situations, we may even be inclined to behave in both ways. We all have good days and bad days; however, the demeanors we choose in any given moment affect the outcome of our conversations, our possibilities, the reactions of others, and how thoroughly we advance toward our goals.

John's Story

John loves being head of a school district, and works to be the best director he can be. However, he still must balance his job with his personal responsibilities. He is a single dad and wants to spend time with his two boys. Numerous tasks at home require his attention, including his thriving vegetable garden. He has many friendships that take time and energy to maintain. How John chooses his priorities affects the quality if his life, the lives of others, and the richness he derives from them.

He's happy with his life, but what if John were unhappy at work or at home? What if he felt dissatisfied or unfulfilled? Should he – or you – keep a job if it is not making us happy? We have a term we call "life giving." Activities that enhance you, help you grow, make a contribution, and/or cause you to feel that you have given well of yourself are life giving. Conversely, the things that shrink you as a person, make you feel less vital, lead to stagnation, or sap your energy undermine your ability to be life-giving.

Is the majority of your time spent in life-giving pursuits? These could be the activities themselves or the way you engage in them. Perhaps the activities are wonderful, but your approach to them drains your life energy. Or maybe your energy is great and you love what you do, but you work with people who are unhappy, selfish, or ungrateful. Surrounding yourself with such individuals could well diminish your own life-giving orientation.

Just as there are infinite points on a circle, there are infinite paths you can take. If you find yourself in a situation that is not life-giving, whether it be at work, in your relationships, or even in how you view yourself, you have the ability to choose to change that situation or the way you behave within it. Here are some practical tips:

- **Remember that small things matter.** Recall the little gestures and acts of kindness others have done for you and that you have done for others. Such acts speak volumes about you, both helping others and making you feel good about yourself. Choose to perform little acts that make a difference and brighten lives, both in the moment and over time.

- **Try on a new attitude.** Commit to walking into the next meeting or having your next conversation with complete grace. Smile and acknowledge people, remembering that you are all on the same team. In fact, walk through your whole day with grace and gratitude for the gifts in your life. See how things turn out.

- **Attend that exercise class you've been meaning to get to.** Rather than getting frustrated about your weight, poor muscle tone, or the flexibility you've lost over the years, go to the gym today and acknowledge yourself for going. Then keep going, and each time acknowledge yourself for your commitment.

- **Research the job or volunteer position of your dreams.** Make lists of all the options you discover within those arenas. Call or e-mail to learn more about these possibilities, and what is involved in making the leap to get there.

Visit FindFulfillFlourish.com and use the card sort exercise to help you identify choices that make your soul sing.

Jerry works for the Department of Corrections, where he encounters hardened criminals as part of his job. On Saturday afternoons in the fall and spring, he helps a very different group of people, coaching youth with disabilities to play various sports and engage in other physical activities. Jerry points out that the two groups are utter opposites. He loves the joy he sees as the kids succeed in challenging themselves and participating in activities many thought were beyond their abilities. He knows he is helping them experience a great sense of accomplishment, which they seem to find very freeing. Jerry chooses to balance the intensity of his work week with an activity that lightens his spirit while bringing light and fun into the lives of special needs youth.

Recognize that every belief, intention, behavior, and impact results from discerning one choice our of many possibilities. How can we make ourselves happy in an unfulfilling situation? How can we gain further fulfillment from an already fulfilling venture? Consider your choices and then recognize that you probably have many additional options. Try a few out. Some may feel ridiculous or unlike you. Others may seem beyond your comfort zone, or even impossible. The idea is to stay open to new possibilities that can take you to new places and become instrumental in helping you create the future you desire. You can be sure of one thing: if you continue doing what you always do, you will get the same results you've always gotten.

Doing nothing is also a choice, and inertia can set in easily. Procrastination can lead to paralysis or create situations that reduce the likelihood of your success. It is imperative, no matter how stuck you feel, to remember that inaction achieves nothing. In doing nothing, you relinquish control and influence over your life to others. You become swept away in the current of life, rather than navigating your stream, and in doing so, you relinquish control over the consequences.

Be brave and take initiative. Break new ground for yourself. If a particular character trait or belief system is on your life-giving agenda, work with it until you boldly demonstrate it. If it is an action or a new work path, explore fully every option you uncover. Stop holding yourself back; give yourself permission to pursue these new choices.

> "If you choose not to decide you still have made a choice."
> — Rush, "Freewill"

Today's Choices Create Our Tomorrows

While our choices certainly affect our future, the only real thing is the present moment. Our future is determined by how willing we are to make the present the best it can be. Our daily, moment-to-moment choices are crucial not only for today, but also for tomorrow, in that today's choices foreshadow the future we will ultimately create.

Examine your life today. Look at what you have, how you feel, your relationships, profession, and the activities you perform in your spare time. Which choices brought you to this point? Your reality today is only a mirror of the choices you have made up to this very moment. Are you satisfied or dissatisfied with them?

Just as your choices yesterday created the reality you have today, the choices you make today will influence tomorrow's reality and every subsequent tomorrow. Since the choices you make today can completely transform your tomorrows, perhaps it is time to make new choices. Be bold. Envision the life you have always wanted. Ask yourself what choices you must make right now to begin to see that life come to fruition. This is the power of choices!

In Chapter 9, "Life Leadership: The First Person You Need to Lead Is Yourself," we introduced the concept of self-leadership and how to lead yourself where you want to go. Your choices define and drive that process. These include the small daily choices you make, as well as the bigger decisions that set the direction and purpose for your life.

Lucie exemplifies a life filled with conscious choice. A teenager, she has been playing violin for many years. Some refer to her as a prodigy. In order to accommodate her need to practice violin five hours a day, she had to gain the cooperation of her school to adjust her class schedule. Lucie's life is filled with practice and performance. But she also is committed to service, recognizing that her music can bring joy and healing to others. Once a week, Lucie volunteers to play violin at local eldercare facilities. She has been doing this for two years. All of Lucie's decisions highlight her choices to be the best she can be, to spread joy and happiness, and to take initiative to lead herself.

To a large degree, you are the sum of your choices and the actions you take to support them. On the following page are some examples:

Everyday Choices

- Doing mostly what you enjoy ... *versus* ... setting priorities and doing what is necessary
- Listening and learning from others ... *versus* ... dismissing the thoughts of others and exclusively presenting your point of view or recommendations

Frame of Mind

- Being grateful for what you have ... *versus* ... being upset or resentful for what you do not possess
- Being honest about yourself ... *versus* ... self-justifying or only seeing what you want to see

Relationships

- Investing time and effort to strengthen and keep relationships healthy and viable ... *versus* ... taking relationships for granted
- Releasing grudges and resentments ... *versus* ... carrying grudges and allowing them to tarnish or destroy relationships

Doing the Right Thing

- Being intellectually honest, truthful, and objective ... *versus* ... spinning facts, creating false impressions or shading the truth
- Acknowledging mistakes and wrongs, being accountable ... *versus* ... ducking responsibility, covering up, denying or blaming

Advocacy and Leadership

- Pursuing a passion actively ... *versus* ... simply talking about a passion
- Having the courage of your convictions ... *versus* ... wilting under pressure

Living Your Life and Your Values

- Adhering to your values even when it may be contrary to your immediate or short-term desires ... *versus* ... acting with expediency or putting immediate self-interests first
- Taking risks to explore new activities and endeavors ... *versus* ... staying within your comfort zone

Doing Your Best

- Taking a challenging route that will likely yield better results ... *versus* ... taking the route of least resistance
- Making a commitment and fulfilling it (keeping promises) ... *versus* ... weaseling out or not fulfilling a commitment fully (breaking promises)

These are just a sample of the big and daily choices we make in our lives. For a more comprehensive list, go to our website, FindFulfillFlourish.com and click on Book & Tools; then click on Supplemental Content.

Choosing Gratitude

Think about something in your life that brings you joy: your work, a relationship, a skill, a hobby, even the roof over your head. Count the things on your list. You may say to yourself, "I really love my ..." This is the beginning of giving thanks to family, friends, nature's abundance, spiritual source, even to your own efforts at bringing these gifts into your life. The result is an immense and powerful feeling of gratitude.

NAVIGATIONAL POINTS

- Our choices define who we are, how we are perceived, and what we make of our lives.
- We choose every aspect of our lives, far more than we may realize.
- Little daily choices matter and accumulate.
- Our collective choices define who we are.
- Learning from our mistakes and changing our behavior are choices.
- Doing nothing is a choice.
- Doing the same thing we've always done will perpetuate the results we already have.
- Others are affected by our choices.
- Our choices reflect our true values.
- Tough choices may become defining moments and can change the trajectory of our lives.

APPLYING THE CONCEPTS TO YOUR LIFE

1. Think about the choices that have led you to where you are today. How much fulfillment are you experiencing as a result?

2. If you are satisfied with your choices, acknowledge yourself. Example: I am proud that I made the decision to join an environmental group.

3. Are you already living a life that gives you joy? If you are less than satisfied, remember that to get different outcomes you will need to make different choices. This will involve breaking old patterns of behavior.

4. Fill in the chart on the next page by listing new choices you will make. Write a goal for implementing each choice, identify challenges you may encounter, and write a benefit you anticipate – for both yourself and others.

MAKING NEW CHOICES

Fill in the chart below by listing new choices you will make. Write a goal for implementing each choice, identify challenges you may encounter, and write a benefit you anticipate — both for yourself and others.

New Choice	Goal	Challenge in Achieving	Benefit

Find a printer-friendly version of this Choices chart at FindFulfillFlourish.com; click on Books & Tools.

flourish

Chapter 11

Passion to Action to Fruition

Building momentum
Designing personal success and fulfillment
Living the journey

Transformation in Action – Making a Difference at Street Level: Tio Hardiman and CeaseFire

Tio Hardiman arrives at his desk early, his first goal of the day to sit down with his "violence interrupters," members of his staff who intercepted last night's shooting. After that, he connects with the outreach workers who tended to the families of those involved in the shooting, as well as their friends and neighbors. During this meeting, he receives a call from an outreach worker employed at the hospital. Last night's victim is going to make it. An angry suture across his entire abdomen will now make him instantly identifiable, but he is one of the lucky ones.

Squeezing in a quick lunch, Tio then heads to meetings with the interfaith clergy who minister to these families. The clergy members' goal is to provide pastoral support and a safe haven; they are now planning the next steps toward greater violence prevention. Tio gets in his car and heads to Chicago's Garfield Park to personally speak with the families and the kids on this neighborhood street, providing his own intervention.

Tio has been on the street with these families for eleven years; the families know and trust him. When none of the two hundred staff members of CeaseFire

Illinois can seem to break through, Tio is there. As the executive director of this nonprofit public health model designed to alleviate bloodshed in violence-plagued communities, Tio is committed to both reducing the brutality and reframing the mindset that fosters it.

A community organizer working in the poverty-stricken neighborhoods of Chicago in the mid-1990s, rallying young men to find alternatives to shooting

> The program is comprised of five components: youth outreach, community mobilization, faith-based leader involvement, public education, and criminal justice participation. All aim to respond to and prevent violent outbreaks.

each other, Tio faced an uphill battle because this was the only reality these young men had ever known. Meanwhile, Dr. Gary Slutkin, an epidemiologist who'd spent most of his previous ten years in Africa working to stop the spread of AIDS, tuberculosis and other contagious diseases, returned home to his native Chicago. Dr. Slutkin was shocked and overwrought to see the amount of violence taking place in his hometown. Dr. Slutkin viewed the violence from a new paradigm: he likened it to an epidemic – an infectious disease that spreads from one person to the next and can be contracted anew at any time. A man of action, Dr. Slutkin knew the epidemic required a cure, so he started the Chicago Project for Violence Prevention. Tio began working with CeaseFire, one of that organization's initiatives, at its inception in 1999.

The program is composed of five components: youth outreach, community mobilization, faith-based leader involvement, public education, and criminal justice participation. All are aimed at responding to and preventing violent outbreaks. Outreach staff members work with high-risk clients who have a history of violence, are known to be weapons carriers, are in gangs, are selling narcotics, or have been released from prison. They build relationships with troubled youths who are susceptible to the violent norms of their streets, facilitating behavior changes by addressing the mindset associated with violence.

Dr. Steven Salzman, a surgeon who sees many of these victims in his emergency room, describes the horrible chain of violence: "The scariest thing is that when these people come in, there is no emotion on their faces. You can *see* them planning their retaliation." The outreach workers strive to reach them while the wounds are still fresh, counseling them against retaliation. The hospital response initiative approaches high-risk youth while they are receiving medical treatment, when they may be more receptive to counseling to change their behavior.

Outreach is a very challenging role, yet it's less direct than the work of the violence interrupters. This is a term Tio Hardiman coined, and a job description he designed in 2004. Tio describes violence interrupters as "streetwise individuals who are familiar with gang life in the communities where CeaseFire is active. Many are former gang members and a number of them have spent time in prison, but they are now on 'this side of the line' and eager to give back and help young people in their neighborhoods." Violence interrupters engage directly with those who carry guns and are prepared to use them. They employ high-risk mediation on a regular basis, with the intention of stopping people from gunning each other down. It's an extremely risky role, but in Tio's world where shootings and stabbings are commonplace, this kind of intervention is absolutely necessary if the cycle of violence is not only to be stopped, but more importantly, prevented.

The second component, community mobilization, includes organizing people in the neighborhoods as emergency and awareness-building response teams, gathering them together when a shooting or other violent act takes place. CeaseFire's commitment is to respond to all violent acts across its fifteen zones within seventy-two hours. "There might be a midnight barbecue where lots of violence had taken place, or we might organize a basketball tournament. We also hold rap sessions, peace summits, and trips out of town to get people away from their violent environment and give them a new perspective," Tio says. "The bottom line is that we increase awareness that violence should not be tolerated anytime, anywhere." The mobilization effort, therefore, goes beyond responding to violence; it is also an educational structure aimed at preventing violent behaviors.

The shootings traumatize everyone they touch. Families are bereaved at the loss of a son, brother, sister, or father. Neighbors grieve the loss of a friend. People feel angry and hurt. To respond to these individuals, CeaseFire's third component engages a cadre of faith-based leaders who volunteer their services to console and pray with those affected by violence. Some churches offer safe havens after hours as alternatives to being out on the street amidst the threat of violence. Other times, families of those touched by the violence need food or clothing. These leaders also offer sites for educational programs aimed at younger siblings.

CeaseFire's one hundred faith-based leaders help meet these needs and others like them. Tio says, "Every faith is represented: Muslim, Catholic, Baptist, Presbyterian, Jewish, Methodist, Lutheran, Evangelist. You name it; we have a faith-based leader that works with CeaseFire. The power of prayer cannot be underestimated in these situations, and the presence of the clergy to listen and provide pastoral care helps reduce the tension when someone has been shot." CeaseFire's clergy members declare peace the norm, not only by their actions in response to violence, but in their commitment to preach peace from their pulpits the first weekend of every month. They regularly encourage their congregations to work for peace, as well.

The public education campaign includes posters, flyers, public service announcements – even buttons – which are distributed to the community, all with the same message about ending the violence. One of CeaseFire's best-known campaigns is a poster of a young boy. It says, "Don't shoot. I wanna grow up." Tio says, "We plaster the city with these posters. Everywhere people look, they see a constant reminder and receive a constant education against violence." Tio and CeaseFire are working to shift this neighborhood's values, which will lead to a cultural transformation. Tio knows this shift is possible, but he also realizes that it will likely evolve slowly, and only with extensive support from individuals who can consistently and visibly demonstrate the other choices and actions possible.

The final component of the program is collaboration with the criminal justice system. "We have a relationship with the police department," Tio notes. "They share data with us so we can compare statistics from one year to the next to see how effective we are at making change. We work together to reduce violence." And CeaseFire has been effective at reducing violence. Police Beat 1115 in West Garfield Park was chosen as the first CeaseFire zone in the year 2000, largely because of the high number of shootings in that community. In CeaseFire's first year, shootings in that neighborhood dropped by 67 percent, a remarkable result.

Tio knows his work is not for everyone; his own background served as a forerunner for his path. "I grew up in the Henry Horner Projects, completely surrounded by violence. I saw people lose their lives, get hurt. I became desensitized to it myself because it was such a part of my everyday life. We became numb in the projects." Tio was a victim of violence as well. "When I was twenty-four, I was cut – stabbed in the back with a big butcher knife when someone tried to rob me. You don't feel the pain right away. Your ego kicks in, and the only thing you can think about is revenge."

Knowing he was on the receiving end of violence, one can't help but wonder: was Tio also a perpetrator of violence? "I've had some close encounters," he admits. "I have never perpetrated violence, but I have acted in self-defense when someone came at me first. Living in the projects, you have to be on the defensive all the time. I navigated pretty well through the concrete jungle.

"But things weren't always bad for me," Tio explains. "My grandparents raised me and put me into Catholic school for grades one through eight. They gave me a good foundation, taught me what was right. Then my grandmother died when I was in eighth grade, and I went to the projects to live with my mother. I remembered the uncles I'd seen at my grandmother's house. They were heroin addicts, and I never wanted to be like them. When I went to the projects, it was so bad. Drugs were everywhere, but I wouldn't do heroin. Instead, I drank, smoked pot, and did cocaine. I lost ten years of my life chasing the cocaine dream.

"When I hit rock bottom in November 1987, I didn't want to renege on all my grandma had taught me. My grandparents were hard-working people, spending long hours in the factories. They put in a lot of sweat to pay for my education, so I felt I had to make something of myself. I went back to school. Looking back on it, it is like I was the Lion King in the Disney movie. I was raised like a lion, but I started hanging out with the hyenas, baboons, and monkeys, and I started acting like them. I had to get back to the greatness of the lions, home to my roots. I had to do the right thing in my life, which was to be a leader, not a follower. The only difference between the Lion King and me is that when I came back to myself, I brought some of the former hyenas and baboons with me." This is compelling evidence of Tio's leadership.

The examples set by Tio's grandparents guided his personal metamorphosis. Even though he got off track, when he hit bottom, the thought of his grandma helped him pull himself out of his life of addiction and create a solid LifePath. Her commitment to him and to his education fueled him. The memory of what his grandparents stood for served as a guide for his directional change.

"I got my associate's degree in 1998, then my bachelor's in 2000. Then I went back to Northeastern University and got my masters degree in 2004." Tio did all of this while employed full-time with CeaseFire. "My first role was as a community coordinator. I did community organizing and established a CeaseFire coalition model that I implemented in two communities. Once I became an employee, I wanted to improve my skill sets." Tio's grandparents were not the only ones who served as exemplars for him: "Dr. Slutkin was my role model. He didn't push me, but I saw him as an artful doctor, in the way he speaks out against violence. He expanded my horizons, and I began to see a bigger picture. That really inspired me and reminded me of my grandparents. I went back to school for my grandma and grandpa."

While Tio was pursuing his education, he was promoted to Director of Mediation Services and Intergovernmental Affairs. His job was establishing relationships with politicians. "When they saw me walking down the street with 500 people, they thought, 'Now that's powerful,' and then they sought me out," Tio remembers. Those political relationships are key in funding the work of CeaseFire and helping spread its message.

Tio kept growing, and as he did, he applied his new knowledge and ideas to CeaseFire. "In 2004, I initiated the violence interrupters into the model. They did great work, and we received a lot of publicity. We were featured in *The New York Times Magazine*. This got me promoted to Director of CeaseFire Illinois." Tio explains that the CeaseFire model has been so successful that it has been replicated in other cities, such as Baltimore, Kansas City, parts of New York State, and Phoenix.

Today, Tio and his wife, Alison, have four children. "We live in a nice neighborhood. I have come a long distance from the projects. My kids hear about the violence in my work; they need not be naïve, and they should not become victims. But my kids are not exposed to the kind of violence I saw when I grew up. I have been able to give them that. My wife gets nervous every now and then, and once in a while, so do the kids. They know that I still do some work on the streets mediating, because people trust me. I don't do as much as I used to. I have trained other people to do the work because I'm getting older and I just can't do it all anymore."

Tio explains, "In Chicago, homicide is the leading cause of death for African American males between the ages of one and thirty-four." That's a startling statistic. Chicago's homicide rate was less than five hundred in 2009, which seems like a big number, until you realize it's down from six hundred sixty-six homicides in 1998, showing that CeaseFire is having an impact. "In 2004, we received state funding for the first time," he continues. "All those talks with politicians paid off. We had a budget of between two and three million dollars allocated to CeaseFire, and we saw a 25 percent reduction in homicides that year, because we intensified our work with the violence interrupters. We were doing really well until our funding was cut in 2007. The government funds enabled us to hire more people. And although CeaseFire is still doing great work, Chicago still holds the second highest homicide rate in the nation. We need more funding so we can put more staff out on the street."

Rather than allowing the slash in his budget to diminish his commitment, Tio has intensified his effort to acquire additional funds. Most of CeaseFire's funding now comes from private foundations, like the Robert Wood Johnson Foundation, Polk Brothers, and the MacArthur Foundation. "We have grant writers on staff," Tio explains, "but government funding is so essential to this work. The more funding we have, the more violence we can prevent." Currently the program is in only 25 percent of the highest-need areas and just 14 percent of the city, overall. If CeaseFire were able to implement a city-wide effort, they project that homicides would fall to fewer than two hundred annually within three years.

Tio articulates his personal vision: "To empower younger people to step into my shoes and take CeaseFire to the next level. I want to move to being the CEO of a foundation like Robert Wood Johnson, Pritzker, or MacArthur, so that I can deal on the resource level and ensure that funding goes to this program. That is the only way we can be truly successful.

"My goal is to change the mindset across America as it relates to violence. When I was a kid, I watched TV and saw movies of cowboys and Indians. In school I learned about Rome, World Wars I and II, and Vietnam, and I saw that violence was a part of everyday life. This is still what our kids see and what they learn, but this is not the way we need to be. I would like to see kids not desensitized to violence, so that they feel safe and secure. I would like to play a crucial role in changing the generations to come so we can live on a more peaceful planet."

Tio is a man of inward and outward transformation. He faced his downward spiraling path and turned it completely around. He got off the street and put himself through rigorous education, reflecting his personal commitment to the values his grandparents instilled in him. He uses his own personal experience as a model for others, demonstrating that they too, can turn their lives around. What more powerful motivator could there be than someone standing in front of you who has surmounted the very challenges you face daily, showing you that change and transformation are indeed possible? Tio has brought this degree of change into his own life, and has made his life's purpose about bringing it into the lives of others. He has put his passion into action.

For further information about CeaseFire Chicago, please visit www.ceasefirechicago.org.

The Work of Change

Changing longstanding behavior patterns requires sustained effort and hard work. Persistence and a commitment to making conscious choices are essential until the new behavior patterns are ingrained into your life. Many great intentions die from the malady of "excusitis" – the tendency to rationalize or excuse away our pattern of discontinuing the effort once it gets challenging and resuming our old ways.

Think about New Year's resolutions. We usually make them with the best intentions, often focusing on the mission of self-improvement. Yet frequently, our commitment to these new behaviors – things like losing weight, quitting smoking, improving our relationships – wanes after just a few weeks. Desire alone is insufficient to manifest change, and it is incredibly easy to slip back into the old, more comfortable, if less healthy, behaviors.

If you've had experiences of failing when trying to make changes in your life, regardless of the arena, you may have reached the point where you believe that change – real change – simply is not possible. This is why so many adults who are dissatisfied with their jobs, for example, choose to remain in the rut rather than go back to school or acquire new skills. Many people, even when unhappy with their lives, view them through the lens of fatalism. "It may be possible for other people to change their circumstances," they think, "but not me. It didn't work last time or the time before. What makes me think that this time I will be able to break through and transform myself?"

Tio Hardiman is certainly an example to all of us about the ability to make an enormous life change. His step-by-step process of moving from a life of addiction on Chicago's streets to his current role as director of CeaseFire shows us how possible even large-scale change is, if we want it badly enough.

External and Intrinsic Motivation

Chances are we can all point to at least one example in our lives where we achieved a certain level of success in making a change. We probably can recall at least one area – if not many areas – where we made positive, lasting changes in our lives. Think of something you learned that took lots of practice. Perhaps it was learning to ride a bicycle, play an instrument, or develop new job skills. At some point during the learning process, you might have said, "How am I ever going to learn this?" Perhaps you gave up temporarily when you hit an obstacle. But somehow, you persevered and eventually reached your goal. While the kind of change you are seeking now may seem much more complex than learning a new task, a combination of external and internal motivational factors apply. Understanding them can help you make long-term changes that lead to greater personal satisfaction in life.

When we begin a new endeavor, we often expect to realize benefits in both the short and long term. Initially, we may receive great feedback about our aims and ideas, meet new people, and feel that we are on the path toward making a positive difference. We may also discover rewards inherent in the process of performing the tasks, activities, and challenges themselves, such as solving problems, working a puzzle, creating something, or mastering new software applications. This is known as intrinsic motivation, an essential element in job satisfaction and in enjoying the pursuit of a purpose.

Then the reality of the undertaking may set in. As we delve further into the process, we may encounter barriers and frustrations which may cause the work to lose some of its initial appeal. The nuts and bolts may feel like drudgery, we may hit a wall in our knowledge, or we may encounter unexpected and perhaps formidable challenges. When that original fascination dissipates, we must rely on our intrinsic motivation and passion to carry us forward.

Ultimately, for a new behavior pattern to become an integral part of your life, and one you are self-motivated to pursue over time, it must eventually become intrinsically reinforcing. This means you need to feel some sense of reward for your accomplishment. It may take the form of personal satisfaction, intellectual stimulation, happiness, emotional well-being, or some other natural feeling that is gratifying or pleasing – which, in turn, increases the likelihood that you will continue your efforts. To reach that place, additional immediate or short-term external reinforcement of your efforts may be necessary. This may come from others you engage, people from whom you seek feedback, or in other ways that provide ongoing encouragement to persevere when the effort becomes overwhelming.

Once your own intrinsic rewards kick in – as you see the progress of your behavior over time – external recognition and rewards will become less important, if not unnecessary, to sustain your momentum. This process is known as conditioning. It is analogous to the way athletes condition themselves physically so they can perform at a higher level. For the purpose of your LifePath, conditioning refers to your process of developing new, sustained patterns of activity. The goal is to plan your actions to condition yourself for success in pursuing your vision.

Because immediate benefits – whether external affirmation, intrinsic motivation, or intrinsic satisfaction – may take time to develop, focus on a future impact and personal rewards must become your driving forces. The chart on the next page will help you distinguish between these three concepts.

External Affirmation

Acknowledgement and reinforcement from others for actions and achievement. Provided initially in our youth, usually by parents, educators, religious leaders, family members, and others. External affirmation becomes reinforcing when it increases the frequency of a behavior.

Intrinsic Motivation

Motivation that stems from rewards inherent in the tasks and challenges we perform, like those experienced when solving a problem, creating something, or mastering software applications.

Intrinsic Satisfaction

The rewarding feeling we experience internally as we see the results of our actions and achievements. This internal sense of fulfillment becomes self-reinforcing and motivates us to continue, even in the absence of external affirmation and reinforcement.

INNER QUEST
Are you more motivated by external affirmation or intrinsic satisfaction?

OUTER QUEST
What steps can you take to achieve self-reinforcing fulfillment?

Doing so will keep your initiative on track, carrying you forward, especially when the initial enthusiasm has waned.

Directional and Habitual Behavior Change

We may desire to make changes that shift or establish a future path. These are directional changes, because they alter or set a new course for our lives. Examples include educational pursuits, career decisions, long-term commitments to causes, and enduring strategic and personal partnerships.

This is the arena in which Tio Hardiman made changes. Seeing himself after ten years as a cocaine addict and then making the decision to change was a significant moment in and of itself. At that point, he had already begun to change his direction. But then Tio had to decide what he wanted to do with his life, and he had to make the necessary preparations – in this case, in his education – to pursue that path effectively.

Habitual change, on the other hand, focuses on altering reoccurring behavior patterns, the ways in which we are accustomed to handling various aspects of our lives. These may be practiced values or actions we have performed for many years, some of which may be positive and constructive. Others – the ones we want to change – are unhealthy or diminish our ability to be the person we want to be. Examples include expressions of anger or exasperation, accusations, jumping to conclusions, making assumptions, overlooking inconvenient

> Directional changes shift or establish a future path. Habitual changes alter recurring behavior patterns.

facts, spinning information, insensitivity, disrespect, intolerance, hidden agendas, overpromising, underperforming, ethical lapses, or the tendency to cut honesty corners. All of these erode trust and credibility, and in the process they undermine our ability to achieve the big things we want to accomplish – including making successful high-priority directional changes.

In Chapter 4, "Values: You Are What You Value," we noted how easy it is to fall into behaviors that are unkind, dishonest, or unjust, and how we may be largely unaware of them until others remark about them and their negative impact. Then, suddenly they become obvious. When we say we value kindness, but are brusque, self-centered, or impatient with people, others may not see us as kind. Making habitual behavior shifts requires a new kind of focus and a conscious self-awareness that allow us to change our lives to accommodate new goals and visions. Habitual behavior patterns involve significant adjustments in how we live and interact, and they are no less important than directional changes. The two work hand-in-hand: constructive habitual behaviors help propel directional change.

New Pathways

When you commit yourself to actively pursuing a purpose – whether is it large or small in scope – you may be choosing a completely new or significantly different path for your life. For example, let's look at some of the people we introduced in prior chapters:

- For Denise Resnik, whose accomplishments we described in Chapter 5, "Inspired Direction: Finding Purpose, Vision, and Action," her

LifePath change was a result of her response to her son's autism, when she founded the Southwest Autism Research & Resource Center.

- For Carolyn Manning, whose story we told in Chapter 6, "Spirituality: If You Breathe, You're Spiritual," her commitment involved founding and spearheading the Welcome to America Project to help refugees settle in America.
- For Kelly Campbell, whose LifePath change we detailed in Chapter 7, "Relationships: Why You Need Others and Others Need You," it entailed changing careers from fashion industry public relations to helping villagers in underdeveloped countries achieve greater self-sufficiency.
- For Yosef Garcia, whose journey we chronicled in Chapter 10, "Choices: Change Your Choices, Change Your Life," his commitment led to a new career devoted to helping Crypto Jews return to the faith of their ancestors.

Each of these individuals created a new purpose and path for his or her life, and in so doing, enriched themselves and others enormously. In order to make such monumental shifts, they committed themselves to life-transforming directional changes. Each had a vision of a better future, which demanded they change their lifestyles, sometimes radically. These choices changed their day-to-day lives and long-term life experiences, proving that change can be healthy even while it may be challenging.

LifePath changes are rich learning opportunities. They entail creating new arenas of achievement, as well as venturing into the personally unknown. While plowing new ground can be filled with uncertainty and anxiety, it can also be energizing and invigorating.

If you have made big changes in your life previously or are continuing on a journey in progress, you may already have developed the skills and behavior patterns needed to succeed. If, however, the idea of making lasting changes is new to you, you may need to adjust your priorities or engage in activities with which you have limited experience or knowledge. The decision to pursue a new path could be a pivotal point in your life's journey.

Pursuing a new, purposeful direction creates opportunities for finding meaning in your life. You will likely encounter unexpected barriers and challenges. Many endeavors are far more complex and involve more work than we might anticipate at the outset. The key is to be mentally prepared to face these obstacles and unpredictable circumstances.

Instantism

The achievements we value most in life usually take time to attain. Think about your education, close relationships, career accomplishments, building your business, or becoming an expert in your field. You achieved each of these over an extended period, one small step building on the next. Attention spans are growing shorter, and it seems that many people today expect to succeed much more quickly, if not instantly. The desire for short-term results often receives priority and greater attention than long-term objectives like building a solid foundation.

On a large scale, we've seen the results of this pattern in recent business failures and economic setbacks. The expectation of quick success, often accompanied by a desire to do less work, seems to be growing further embedded into our culture. The problem is that this "I want it now" philosophy is a prescription for great frustration and disappointment, since most of the time, it runs counter to reality, and eventually the bubble bursts.

We can speculate on the genesis of this instantism. Perhaps it began with television, where big problems are routinely solved in one-hour episodes. It might have been perpetuated by the amazing new technologies that have become such an integral part of our lives. We used to be quite satisfied to mail a letter across the country, which might have taken four or five days to arrive, and wait another few days for a reply. Then overnight express delivery and faxes became the norm, and the expectation for a reply shrank to a day or two. Now, with e-mail and text messaging, we can reach someone in an instant. We can send documents and photos to friends, family, customers, colleagues, and just about anyone in a far off city with the click of a mouse. We can research any topic on the Internet in seconds, rather than spending hours in the library.

Today's young people are growing up in this culture, and all of us are exposed to it through television and other media: lose weight in thirty days, build muscles fast, get your degree online practically overnight. We've become a culture that seems to demand instant satisfaction. One teenager recently comment-

> "Great things are not done by impulse, but by a series of small things brought together."
> — Vincent van Gogh

ed, "When I text one of my classmates to ask with help for a school assignment, if I don't get a reply within thirty seconds, I know he just doesn't want to do it." While this may sound extreme, it clearly reflects the short-term expectations many are developing in this era of instantism.

The innovations of our day make it possible to do more in less time than in the past; however, few – if any – shortcuts exist to attaining the intrinsically rewarding and highly valued accomplishments that are truly meaningful. These take time, along with sustained and committed effort. It is important for us to recognize that although technology instantly puts many things at our fingertips, the kind of personal fulfillment that grows from living a meaningful life and pursuing a purpose-driven journey cannot be texted or downloaded in an instant.

It is likely that the accomplishments you most value or of which you are most proud were not achieved in a moment, but resulted from a deep investment of yourself, your energy, and your resources. You may have had to work through conflicts, gain new skills, and stretch beyond what you thought was possible. Nevertheless, you achieved your goal through persistence and conviction. The same principles apply to your LifePath and the process of transforming your inspiration into reality.

Consider Tio Hardiman for a moment. Once he shifted out of his addiction, he began working as a community organizer and attracted the attention of Dr. Slutkin. He started in Dr. Slutkin's organization as an entry-level employee and discovered how to emulate the qualities of the man who had hired him. Tio realized that if he wanted to elevate himself as an employee of CeaseFire, the only way to do that would be through his own hard work. The choices he made earned him success and became the foundation he needed to keep moving forward. None of Tio's desires could have been completed in an instant. His commitment to his purpose drove him to continue his education for many years before seeing the fruit of his efforts.

Two Types of Higher Level Self-Interest

Earlier, we discussed the role of self-interest. Again, self-interest is not an inherently bad thing. ***Enlightened self-interest*** involves putting the interests of others ahead of your own, with the expectation that ultimately your personal interests and needs will be fulfilled as well. You understand up front that the personal rewards and satisfaction you seek may be deferred.

Sarah, the young woman you met in Chapter 2, "The Journey to Find Meaning and Become a 'Heartisan,'" offers an excellent description of the concept of enlightened self-interest. She explains that some of what she receives from her many community and social service activities is personal fulfillment and excitement. Her involvement makes her feel good about herself and inspires her to do more. Additionally, Sarah knows that her volunteer work will strengthen her college applications, and that it has transformed her into an acknowledged leader. For example, Sarah was selected to give her high school graduation address. For her, there is a difference between potential self-interest and knowing one's purpose. Personally benefiting from community service does not make it a selfish act. This distinction gets to the heart of enlightened self-interest.

A second type of higher self-interest is ***indirect self-interest***. While related to enlightened self-interest, it has its own distinguishing characteristics. This concept refers to situations in which people are motivated to work for a cause because they believe the changes they help implement have the potential to benefit them indirectly. For example, an initiative to improve educational opportunities will strengthen a community, and the community members engaged in that effort, as well as their children, stand to benefit indirectly.

Both enlightened self-interest and indirect self-interest are key motivators in sustaining the journey to personal fulfillment and a meaningful life. Additionally, both are instrumental in building or transforming long-term and continual behavioral patterns. Shorter-term and intermediate affirmations, along with reaching milestones along the way, help fuel persistence. Ultimately, the gratification from the intrinsic rewards may mean the most and may take the longest to realize.

The process of transforming inspiration into your LifePath is likely different for each individual. Knowing what you find rewarding or reinforcing, from both internal and external sources, can help you chart your path and ensure that you continue to experience the personal satisfaction necessary to keep moving forward. Use your knowledge of what you find reinforcing – things that increase the likelihood that you will engage in activities that further your journey – in designing your path, so you can experience these rewards as you make progress. These reinforcers may be social in nature, emanating from the other people around you, or stem from self-recognition and celebrations as you achieve milestones and tangible outcomes.

Staying the Course

Besides giving you a direction for your LifePath, having a vision also serves as a beacon that keeps you on track when you are at risk of falling prey to excusitis or succumbing to fear of failure. To improve your likelihood of staying the course, write out your vision, using clear, simple, and inspiring words to define it. Carry a copy with you and post it in prominent places. Ask people you trust to remind you of this vision when the going gets tough. Reminding yourself of your vision may be one of the easiest and most powerful exercises to help you maintain and strengthen your resolve or transform your behavior.

> The key to rebounding from setbacks is to gain what you can from the experience and then leave it in the past.

It's virtually a sure thing that you will experience setbacks as you pursue your LifePath. You can view these challenges as blockades, or as tools that can make you stronger and even more determined. They can also be the wellspring from which wisdom develops. Wisdom is something we attain from accumulated life experience, trial and error, and experimenting with guidance from others. When we refer to reversals in progress as setbacks – not failures – they simply become temporary detours.

The key to rebounding from setbacks is to gain what you can from the experience and then leave it in the past. When we allow past mistakes to haunt us in the present, we inhibit our ability to create the future we most desire. Neither Tio Hardiman nor Tim Lewis could have accomplished what they did if they had remained rooted in their past mistakes. Give yourself the freedom to pursue new possibilities with a positive focus on the future.

Setbacks often occur because we make errors or misjudge situations, or because unanticipated events interfere with our progress. As humans, we all make mistakes, usually lots of them. As if that's not enough, we may carry around the burdens of these mistakes, punishing ourselves unnecessarily or living with regret. This is always a waste of time and energy. As Steve's mother-in-law, Shirley Kabin, a former dancer and choreographer, would say, "You need to dust yourself off, pick yourself up, wipe off your hands, lift your head, and keep stepping."

Developing an Action Plan

A plan is essential for transforming your inspiration and purpose into a LifePath, especially if you would like it to be more than a solo effort or string of random activities. Many different types of plans exist, depending on your specific goals. For example, a strategic plan articulates your vision and long-term direction, defines your purpose or mission, and delineates how you will achieve success by creating a multi-year process, setting priorities, and allocating resources. This may be something to tackle when you have determined the scope of your endeavor. Strategic plans are implemented though shorter-term and more tactical action plans.

A good action plan is an effective tool for setting priorities, organizing tasks, staying on track, and refocusing when detours occur. The key is to follow the plan and update it as you move along. We suggest beginning with an action plan if you are just getting under way, and building momentum accordingly. Eventually, you will graduate to a longer-term, more strategic plan, depending on the scope of your endeavor. We recommend this approach as you immerse yourself in your journey because you may be climbing a fairly steep learning curve. The new information and knowledge you gain will enable you to develop a realistic, achievable strategic plan to further guide your success.

Your purpose defines your reason for action, your vision defines what success looks like, and your action plan serves as a road map for moving forward. Progress is about the route and methods, rather than the destination. The important thing is to identify your goals and plan how you will achieve them.

Visit FindFulfillFlourish.com and click on Book & Tools for a diagram of how these pieces work together.

Putting your action plan into motion and taking the steps to achieve your goals is one of three key implementation phases in manifesting your vision. It is also important to evaluate your progress, identifying what has gone well and what hasn't quite worked. Your next step is to solve problems and determine where you can make improvements. You then loop back to the planning process. Midcourse adjustments may be necessary that affect the goals, activities, resources, and timelines you had initially set. If this is the case, you will need to revisit certain components of your plan, and update the plan to reflect the new realities. Remember, setbacks are merely delays, and sometimes fortuitous discoveries arise from changes in plans or timelines.

Creating an action plan is a straightforward process. It entails laying out all the elements involved in moving forward. Most action plans include information about:

- Specific goals
- Action steps
- Milestones
- Timelines
- Measurements
- People to engage
- Resources to deploy
- Potential challenges
- Ways to address challenges
- Contingency plans

Use the template on the following page to create your action plan. Visit FindFulfill-Flourish.com and click on Book & Tools for a printable version.

Your plan need not be elaborate. Use this as a tool for thinking through the steps to make your vision a reality. Once you have completed your plan, it will serve as a daily reminder of your goal and the steps needed to accomplish that goal. Remember to continually update it as you make progress and new discoveries.

Contingency Plans

A contingency plan, also famously known as "Plan B," is a safeguard against potential setbacks. It is a back-up plan for use as an alternative when you need to start over in a certain area. Having a realistic one in place can help in you rebound quickly. Being prepared with a good Plan B is a smart practice, especially in situations where there is significant uncertainty about whether the initial approach will generate the desired results. Consider your contingency plan an insurance policy to help minimize potential losses. When much is at stake, a back-up is prudent to prevent the potential waste of time and resources.

Checklists: Chunking Down Activities

One barrier to success for many people is setting goals that, while inspiring, are too big to tackle all at once. Take the example of Elaine Birks-Mitchell

ACTION PLAN FOR EACH GOAL

GOAL — What is to be achieved?

Action Steps	Milestones	Timeline	Measurements	People to Engage	Resources	Possible Challenges
How will the goal be achieved? What is the sequence of activities?	*What are the key markets or stages of completion?*	*When will it be complete? What is the deadline?*	*How will you know a specific step or goal has been achieved?*	*Who will be involved and responsible?*	*What financial, human, and other resources are needed? What is your budget?*	*Which barriers or resistance might you encounter/ How will you get past them?*

Find a printer-friendly version of this worksheet at FindFulfillFlourish.com. Click the Books & Tools tab and then Additional Application Exercises.

and her bra recycling business. Elaine's first thought was of her desire to serve. She believed there must be some use for her old bras. By combining her ideas, research, what she knew of vulnerable women, and calls to women's shelters, she had a beginning. As soon as Elaine saw the traumatized women with little to call their own, her vision crystallized: that no woman in a shelter or experiencing economic strife should lack a well-fitting, supportive bra. Elaine sees a good bra as a metaphor for the way a woman walks in the world.

Elaine realized that achieving her goal would require many steps. In her first year she was able to donate 20,000 bras. While that sounds like an enormous number, it is a mere stitch in the voluminous fabric of her vision. Accomplishing her massive goal will require donations from friends, coworkers, church members, and all of their friends – everyone she can think of. She also needs donations from bra manufacturers and stores. Reaching out to all of these people is a huge undertaking, especially for a woman who has a husband and a full-time job, in addition to her bra recycling work.

Breaking her project down into small action steps helped Elaine plan and implement it successfully:

1. She first researched women's shelters in her community, and began to get a sense of the need.

2. She then set an objective to solicit the people she knew for donations.

3. Elaine launched her initial campaign to solicit bras within the local community.

4. She created a process for gathering, organizing, storing, and distributing the bras.

5. As Elaine made headway, she discovered she could export bras, which would provide her with financing to offer other bras as a donation. This added a significant new dimension to her endeavor.

6. She then identified these exporters.

7. Her next step was to research the names and contact information of bra manufacturers.

8. Elaine researched bra stores and lingerie departments in larger stores that might be willing to donate overstock or clearance items.

9. She made a plan to contact these companies.

10. Bit by bit, she reached out to every contact in the steps above.

Of course, additional steps followed.

If Elaine had focused on the enormity of the project, she could easily have become overwhelmed. However, her ability to break the big project into small pieces allowed her to set goals and tackle each task as her schedule permitted, only moving on to the next when she was ready.

Like Elaine, you can break your project down into small action steps and plan to tackle them one task at a time. This will make the process of realizing your vision more manageable. Your vision may take years to achieve, depending on its scope; if it is a vast vision, it is possible that you will not see it fully achieved in your lifetime. However, if you break the process into discrete pieces with clear start and finish points, they will build on one and other, and you will begin to see concrete results. Your intermediate successes lead to the full realization of your vision. Begin by identifying your goals and the steps for achieving each, and prepare an action plan. You will then have a road map for the next leg of your journey, and be on your way to transforming your inspiration into your LifePath.

Role Models, Mentors and Coaches

As we discuss in Chapter 7, "Relationships: Why You Need Others and Others Need You," role models are invaluable as guiding examples for the pursuit of your purpose and vision. They can also be ongoing sources of inspiration as you travel your LifePath journey. This person may be a leader in your field, someone whose values you admire and respect, someone who has reached a certain level of accomplishment, or someone who made a contribution you wish to emulate.

A role model can be someone you know or someone you've never met. It might be one of your parents, a sports figure, the head of your business, a religious or political figure, a volunteer in your community, or even a close friend. It could be a historical figure from the recent or distant past. This figure can be a guiding light, inspiring you on your path, as well as helping you maintain your commitment when you find yourself confronting obstacles or challenges.

Tio Hardiman's first role models were his grandparents, though he was well into his adult life before he recognized this and acted on it. Once he did, their values guided him constantly. When Tio met Dr. Slutkin, he discovered that the doctor, too, was a role model. Two things that impressed Tio about Dr. Slutkin were how knowledgeable he was and his ability to use that learning for good. Education is a core value for all of Tio's role models.

The process of transforming your passion to action and then to fruition on your LifePath may be fraught with unexpected twists and turns. This may be especially true if you are embarking on a project that requires you to master new skills or information. A mentor or coach can offer you the benefit of his or her experience, expertise, and insight. Such a relationship can be crucial to navigating issues, overcoming barriers, planning your process, and providing guidance on various matters. Other people often view our circumstances with an objective eye and can see what we cannot because we are so close to the issues. Someone with a more detached perspective, who has perhaps tread a similar path, can help us navigate our path so that we can avoid setbacks or quickly rebound from them when they occur.

Your coach or mentor may be someone who works with you for no cost, or it may be someone you pay. You might already know someone who could serve in this role. You might also find someone through a referral. Or you may need to be more creative and seek a mentor or coach through other means. Perhaps you know of an organization whose vision is similar to yours; you may find a mentor through that affiliation. You might also use the Internet to find an appropriate guide. Take care to do some research about anyone you meet online, asking for references and a résumé.

The value of a mentor is incalculable in that such a person can help you grow in any number of areas critical to your success. This individual may also serve as an important support system, helping you to understand certain difficulties in your process, coaching you when the chips are down, and most importantly, rallying behind you and your vision.

Reinforcing Your Own Behavior

Often when we are young, many people reinforce our choices and actions. Our parents may praise us when we learn to tie our shoelaces or make our bed. Our teachers may commend us for doing well in spelling, math, or art. Our clergy may acknowledge us for asking insightful questions or performing a kind act for a fellow congregant. Sometimes we receive positive feedback, while other times we receive rewards like money, gifts, or a special outing. When these rewards lead us to repeat the behaviors, they have reinforced the behaviors. At some point, however, praise for tying our shoes or rewards for performing other tasks is no longer necessary or appropriate; the behaviors and their outcomes have become intrinsically reinforcing. We now have the ability to reinforce ourselves – we can acknowledge and reward ourselves for our own actions and accomplishments.

The way people reinforce themselves varies, because we each find different things rewarding. Some may prefer tangible rewards, such as a nice meal as a reward for hitting a goal. For someone else, a long bubble bath is the perfect reward. For another, a ticket to a ball game is a great bonus for work well done.

On the other hand, intangible reinforcements may be the most personally profound. You can become the voice of praise inside your own head, the one who says to yourself, "I did a great job. I am proud of myself. I reached an important goal and overcame obstacles along the way. Good for me!" As you transform your inspiration into a LifePath, you may experience a deep, personal sense of fulfillment and gratification. This may be the most meaningful aspect of your journey.

While you pursue your purpose and passion, your ability to self-reinforce and experience the intrinsic rewards of your work will propel your journey. This may be coupled with acknowledgment or reinforcement from others who provide additional affirmation and external validation. However, there will be times when no one else notices your triumphs. There may be times when the people around you fail to fully understand your commitment to your LifePath. You may find yourself greatly frustrated when it seems that the rewards are few and far between. In these moments, your ability to self-reward will give you the strength necessary to push through to the next goal.

The Inside Impact of LifePath GPS

A more purposeful life is almost invariably a more rewarding life. In some ways, it is a journey of self-discovery that will shape a key part of your identity. You may find that you feel more grateful for your talents and gifts and your ability to use them to make a positive difference. You may notice yourself smiling more. This is the kernel of personal fulfillment, the feeling that you have done something worthwhile with your day. Days turn into weeks, weeks into months, and months to years. At some point you will look back on your choices and see that they have truly enhanced your life and that your cumulative actions are bearing fruit. You are on your LifePath.

You may notice other changes in your life as well. They may be less tangible, but equally significant. When you commit to pursuing your LifePath, you bring forth the best aspects of who you are, what some refer to as "your best self." In the spiritual world, this is referred to as "your divine self." You may have experienced this state often, from time to time, or not at all. Much like enlightened self-interest that works to benefit others, a cause, or a community, your better self is able to step beyond the everyday busy-ness, into a higher place of spirit. This can even be a place of holiness.

When you initially reach this state, you may not recognize it; however, in time, you may notice that you are kinder, more patient, more sympathetic, or more loving. When you act to realize your passion bring it to fruition, and guide your life's journey, you may find yourself truly transformed.

Robin's and Steve's Personal Transformations

Robin chose to become a rabbi late in life, after years of work in the alternative health care field.

I always enjoyed caring for people, but my study to become a rabbi engaged me in a way that was far beyond anything I had ever done before. Not only was the task intellectually demanding, but it caused me to create a spiritual discipline that was unprecedented in my previous ventures. I particularly mean the way I lived my life with respect to my values. It involved the way I related to every individual I met. My religious studies forced me to challenge my own impatience, shortness of temper, and high standards, for example.

Simultaneously, I became aware of each person as divine: the maintenance worker cleaning the hall, the food service staff in the cafeteria, the elderly woman crossing the street. The maintenance man now has a name, John. He emigrated to the United States from the Ukraine as a boy and now had two grown children. He was as loyal as could be and would watch your possessions like a hawk if you had to step away. Manuel in the cafeteria always has a smile on his face. Santo is the fastest omelette cook around, yet he is soft-hearted if you can catch him when the line is slow. The elderly woman crossing the street, Irma, came over from Russia thirty years ago. Her English is still very weak, and she has no car. Her husband is gone, and she lives alone. At age sixty-eight she looks at least ten years older, yet she still takes care of herself.

Each person is no longer just another body in a busy city, but an individual filled with hopes, dreams, needs, fears, loves, and a family to care for. Each one has become a reflection of God's supreme and awesome power and an expression of divine uniqueness. This transformation in my outlook occurred over time and took special effort. Once I recognized that my call to the rabbinate was a result of seeing God in all things and creatures, I had to express this in the way I related to every individual in my life.

This work goes on. Certain days, I find myself impatient or tested. Steve and I would be disingenuous if we told you that behavior changes were easy or something that could be accomplished permanently, within a predefined period of time. Precisely because we are human, we are flawed. It is our commitment to both make the world a better place and to improve ourselves in the process that keeps us going. The two are inextricably intertwined.

Steve also has experienced significant changes in his life and purpose. His changes occurred in one big shift, and then more degree by degree.

For nearly fifteen years, I worked for organizational and human resources development consulting firms, the last several as a vice president. I was traveling throughout the United States, and also internationally, at times. Airplane flights afforded me the opportunity to reflect on my life and the contributions I was making to the greater good, as well as to note the toll that so much travel was exacting on my family.

One day, it occurred to me that I was applying all my work and expertise to helping large corporations, yet thousands of nonprofit organizations could benefit from my skills and expertise. But the nonprofits could not afford the fees the large firms charged. I made a mental note that I would someday find a way to give back. I also made a personal commitment that "someday" would be sooner, rather than later or never.

One Friday, I returned from a business trip and discovered that life at home was out of kilter. I was exhausted. My travel schedule meant I was away from home for 80 percent of the work week. My wife, who had her own stressful job and a fourty-five-minute commute in heavy, rush-hour traffic, also was exhausted. Our son, who was in first grade at the time, was attending before- and after-school programs while his parents were occupied with their jobs – and he was clearly unhappy. Even during the small amounts of time we spent together as a family, no one was at their best.

I knew something had to change and I felt it had to start with me. Yet I felt consumed by my job responsibilities. My wife crystallized the issue when she said to me, "On your tombstone, it will not say 'loyal employee of …'" That's when I fully realized that I had to put my family first, in both word and deed. Over the next three months, I phased out of my job and chose to become an independent consultant, while also working with a local colleague, all of which opened up time and opportunity to begin giving back.

Over the next few months, our family life improved dramatically, and I sought opportunities to become engaged with local nonprofit organizations. I consulted informally – gratis – for a number of social benefit organizations whose missions focused on education, combating discrimination, and inspiring inner-city elementary children from economically disadvantaged households. I discovered that my purpose was helping social benefit organizations become more effective in defining and achieving their goals. This continues to be my focus, both as a volunteer and as a professional – and I make my services affordable to organizations with tight budgets. This book is a natural extension of my purpose, guiding others to develop a greater purpose, live more fulfilling lives, and generate benefits that will make a difference.

Change and Personal Growth

What both of our stories have in common is that our LifePaths changed, and as a result, we grew. Some of the changes were apparent in an instant, while others evolved over years. For those that took time to unfold, markers along the way showed us that we were indeed changing, encouraging us onward. While we were in the midst of the process, the change was not always apparent. Sometimes it is difficult to step back from yourself and see the progress you are making. The process is often messy and unclear, but at some point you will look back and notice changes have indeed occurred. You will see the fruits. Persistence and focus on your ultimate goal will lead to the transformation you seek. It may be dramatic and life-changing or, like most of us, you may continually walk that path to self-improvement, recognizing that the journey to fulfillment is a lifelong process.

In some moments, the work of moving from passion to action to fruition is easy. Seeing someone benefit directly from your generosity or commitment is like food that fuels your journey of personal development and fulfillment. These are the ice cream moments – you are sure you are on the right path and you know you have touched someone else's life. In other moments, the work seems grueling. You may be tired and stressed due to personal concerns, or battling with people who don't see the value of your vision. They may not understand that working for the good of others is also a way caring for themselves. While each of us must take personal responsibility, we share this one planet and all the resources it provides.

Isaac Newton taught us that every action has an equal and opposite reaction. While these reactions may be easily visible in the physical world, they can be much more subtle in the social, interpersonal, service, and political worlds. Each of our actions impacts others, even if we can't immediately see how. That impact may be beneficial or detrimental. When you appreciate this fact, but those around you seem oblivious of Newton and his equal and opposite reactions, pursuing your purpose can become extremely challenging. Taking the high road may seem more trouble than it's worth – or you may react negatively in a moment of overwhelm.

Though the goal for your LifePath is to be your best possible self, it is important that you refrain from reprimanding yourself for your humanness. Recognizing that you've exhibited behavior that is out of alignment with your values is important and will help you to learn, realign, and improve next time.

Have compassion for yourself. We all make mistakes and fall short of our goals at times. Accepting this will make your path to self-fulfillment much more joyful and successful. One day you will wake up and realize that you've become more of the person you wanted to be. It won't be the end of the road, but you will have discovered a you that is closer to your vision for the world.

Personal Convictions

Your personal convictions constitute a belief system that guides your decisions and your life. They represent important truths to which you are devoted.

In a sense, they are your moral code. People with courageous convictions adhere to them, even in challenging situations or when under pressure to compromise them. They hold even faster to these convictions when adverse consequences might result. Others admire these people and view them as role models, largely because of their exemplary strength of character, particularly when they could face personal loss as a result. History is replete with examples:

- Abraham Lincoln encountered strong opposition to his convictions about the immorality of slavery and the indivisibility of the country. He prevailed in ending slavery by signing the Emancipation Proclamation, winning the American Civil War, and preserving the Union.

- Susan B. Anthony became an American civil rights activist at the age of sixteen, and continued until her retirement at age eighty. She advocated for equal rights for African-Americans and women and founded the National Woman Suffrage Association. Opposition to voting rights for women prevailed until fourteen years after her death, with the passage of the 19th Amendment to the United States Constitution.

- Mohandas Karamchand Gandhi, India's foremost spiritual and civil leader during the Indian independence movement between 1915 and 1945, resisted British rule by leading exercises in nonviolent civil disobedience, often jeopardizing his own safety and freedom. His values of nonviolence, freedom, modesty, and simplicity have made him an international role model for peaceful change.

- Margaret Thatcher, Prime Minister of the United Kingdom from 1979 to 1990, substantially improved Great Britain's economy after years of decline. She was a strong believer in free markets, less government regulation of financial markets, privatization of state enterprises, reducing the power of labor unions, lower taxes, and entrepreneurship. She faced strong opposition from entrenched interests, yet prevailed in advancing her principles and policies, which created long-term gains for the people of Britain.

- Nelson Mandela, President of South Africa from 1994 to 1999, served twenty-seven years in prison for his anti-apartheid activity and role in the African National Congress. The first South African president elected in a democratic election, Mandela promoted reconciliation and negotiation to heal the nation's wounds, and facilitated the country's transition to a multiracial and inclusive democracy in spite of strong opposition from many of his supporters.

These famous leaders lived by their strong convictions, as do many everyday people who are making a difference in their communities, if on a smaller scale. Their example reminds us how much it matters that you take a stand for your beliefs and express your values and convictions through your actions.

Zuhdi Jasser, whom you met in Chapter 4, "Values: You Are What You Value," is one of thousands of such role models. He, like so many others, began by expressing his convictions and demonstrating them through his actions in his own community. He then established the American Islamic Forum for Democracy, and his influence grew. He continues to follow his moral code, focusing his LifePath on the greater good, rather than on personal, short-term gains, with the objective of bringing his vision to fruition. We can learn as much from Zuhdi's convictions as we can from Lincoln, Anthony, Gandhi, Thatcher, and Mandela.

People who lack convictions, or whose behavior seems to run counter to what they proclaim, can be viewed as rudderless – lacking direction, unpredictable, and sometimes hypocritical or duplicitous. Remaining true to your convictions is a critical element in transforming your commitment and vision into a healthy LifePath and future reality.

Carolyn Manning repeatedly noted how pursuing her vision tested her on so many levels. She was an independent person and hated asking people for help. Yet her purpose caused her constantly to ask: for donations, for time, for use of a

WHY SHOULD YOU CARE?

Two men are fishing together in a small boat. One man starts throwing his loose, smelly garbage under his seat. His partner asks him, "What are you doing?"

The first man replies, "I'm tossing my trash."

"Can't you put it in a bag?" asks his friend.

"It's my seat," says the first. "Why should you care what I do at my seat?"

A few hours later, the second man pulls out a hand drill. Placing the bit on the wooden floor under his feet, he begins to turn the handle. The first man jumps with alarm: "What are you doing!?"

The second says, "I'm drilling a hole."

"Are you crazy?" screams the first.

His friend looks at him and says calmly, "This is my seat. Why should you care what I do at my seat?"

strong back or a truck in which to deliver furniture. Carolyn also had to constant-ly overcome the suspicion and the cultural norms that made her an outsider to the very people she wanted to befriend. Yet she persisted, largely because her of belief in the value of her work. Her convictions became her driving force.

We encourage you to say "Yes" to the dream, and "No" to the obstacle. This re-quires conviction, persistence, modeling your values, taking action, and seizing the

INNER QUEST
What are your personal convictions?

OUTER QUEST
How do you demonstrate them?

day, all key parts of life leadership. Start with your conviction, and hold your vi-sion in spite of the obstacles. In fact, standing stronger in the face of obstacles, as Zuhdi Jasser and Carolyn Manning did, will enable you to push through the barriers and take the next step toward achieving your vision and inspiring others.

The Tree Metaphor

The tree is a powerful metaphor for the work in this book. Our ideals and goals are like the branches and leaves of a tree that reach up to the sky. The only way the tree's branches can reach upward is if it has a very strong set of roots that anchor it. Your passion and vision, along with the accompanying goals and ben-efits, are the branches and leaves that stretch you upward. They are your higher purpose, elevating you and those around you to a higher place. The roots are your anchors, things like your values, purpose, spirituality, and the relationships that keep you going. Coupled with your convictions and internal reinforcement, the roots help you stay your course.

Nevertheless, we must remember that a mighty oak or redwood was not always sturdy and well established. First, it had to pass through many seasons of growth. A sapling does not become a strong tree overnight; in its youth, it is vulnerable. It can become uprooted and is more susceptible to over- or under-watering than an adult tree. Too much or too little sun will affect its growth. Its location also plays a role. Trees in the forest are shielded against adverse conditions by the canopy of other trees. However, a tree planted in the open frequently needs stakes to support it until its root system matures enough for it to remain upright. In time, the stakes are removed and the tree proudly grows, able to stand on its own, even in gusty conditions.

The same is true regarding our goals and visions: we must first establish the roots of our purpose and values. Relationships may serve as ancillary roots to support us. They may be our stakes as we chart our course while our own roots grow. Trees represent incredible hope. In order to continue to grow and flourish, their roots need tending with appropriate nutrients. People require the same.

Take time to study some trees, both young and old, the saplings and the great majesties in your neighborhood or a nearby forest. Note the differences between the young trees and the established ones. Regardless of where you are on your journey, you can become a strong, healthy tree through your vision and behaviors. Root yourself well and give yourself the supports you need for your journey – and bring your passion to fruition by transforming your inspiration into reality and a LifePath.

NAVIGATIONAL POINTS

- Transforming your inspiration to a LifePath involves translating your passion into actions, which may entail significant changes in your life.
- Identify what motivates and reinforces you from both external and internal sources, and integrate these into your plan and process.
- Enlightened self-interest and indirect self-interest can be strong motivational forces.
- Directional and habitual behavior changes are synergistic – they interact, and when they are aligned, they work together to produce greater results.
- A journey along a new purpose-guided pathway requires sustained commitment.
- The accomplishments we value most usually take time and substantial effort to achieve.
- We develop wisdom from our life experiences, especially as we learn from our mistakes.
- Rebound from setbacks. Dust yourself off, get back up, and keep stepping.
- Prepare an action plan for your project and hold yourself accountable.

- Stand for your convictions; they represent your belief system and moral code.
- Create opportunities to appreciate your successes internally.
- Your LifePath, like a tree, represents incredible hope, as well as the need for sustained nurturing.

APPLYING THE CONCEPTS TO YOUR LIFE

1. What external things, people, situations, and events motivate or appeal to you?
2. What hooks you intellectually and emotionally?
3. What energizes you and makes you feel good inside?
4. What are some of your enlightened self-interests?
5. What are some of your indirect self-interests?
6. What are your other self-interests?
7. What are some of the challenges you anticipate with regard to making directional changes in your life? How can you adjust to meet those challenges?
8. What are some of the challenges you anticipate when it comes to making habitual changes in your life? How can you adjust to meet those challenges?
9. What are your key personal convictions? How are these convictions important to achieving your purpose?
10. How else can your convictions benefit you in achieving your purpose?

Worksheets and supplemental exercises for "Passion to Action to Fruition" are available at FindFulfillFlourish.com. Click on Book & Tools.

Chapter 12

Forward Navigation: Who Am I Becoming?

Defining your Beliefs, Intentions, Behavior, and Impact (BIBI) to create a unique personal identity

Weaving your BIBI into the Eight Dynamics of your LifePath

Moving forward with a clear direction

ind Fulfill Flourish is about an incredible journey to make your life as meaningful and fulfilling as possible. It's about purpose, passion, heart, and direction, and the use of these elements to navigate your future so you can flourish in your own unique way.

Early in the book, we cited a passage from Lewis Carroll's *Alice's Adventures in Wonderland*, in which Alice asks, "Who in the world am I?" Answering this question for yourself is an important element in developing a fulfilling life. If you do not know who you are, how can you fulfill your life's purpose? This chapter is largely devoted to providing guidance and insight for answering this essential question.

Answering the Question "Who are You?" (and Who am I?)

Who are you? This is simultaneously one of the simplest and one of the most perplexing of all questions. Philosophers and theologians have debated the answer to this question for centuries. Some speak to its complexities as they relate to the dynamics of life. Theologians often focus on spiritual and divine aspects of the answer. Other scholars discuss the physical nature of our bodies and form. Psychologists explore identity and identity crises, personality, personal motivations, and emotional characteristics. Educators tend to focus on interests, abilities, and activities. Each of these approaches focuses on different and overlapping aspects of WHO we are. Much of this conversation is abstract, theoretical, and intangible – none of it fully capturing the reality of our daily lives and how we got to this point.

BELIEFS

INTENTIONS

BEHAVIOR

IMPACT

Many people, when asked, "WHO are you?" discuss WHAT they are. They mention their job, education, marital status, age, stature, physical abilities, and parenting status. While all of these are important aspects of our life in this complex world, the WHO question is more about our character, and less about our titles or descriptions.

WHO you are is a composite of your Beliefs, Intentions, Behavior, and Impact (BIBI). And WHO you are will change as these concepts change. Ultimately, each of us needs to answer the question "Who am I?" for ourselves in our own unique way.

The first two parts of BIBI, beliefs and intentions, refer to your inner state. Beliefs are comprised of your thoughts, feelings, convictions, faith, and values. Intentions lean toward your motivations and purposes. Together, these form your "heart" – your emotional and intellectual center.

The second half of BIBI, behavior and impact, are the outward expression of your beliefs and intentions. These consist of your actions and their outcomes. The more your behaviors and impact are aligned with your beliefs and intentions, the truer you are to yourself. That's when the inner WHO and the outer WHO become one – or as close to one as possible. As imperfect beings, we will probably never be fully aligned, but we can do our best to achieve this inner and outer integration – and when we do, our heart truly shines through.

WHO you are in others' eyes is determined by how you express your being in the world – your behavior and impact. Based on their observations, others tend to develop assumptions about your inner depths: your beliefs and intentions.

The four aspects of BIBI are integrated and embedded into the fabric of the Eight Dynamics: (1) your vision and purpose, (2) the values you live, (3) your choices, (4) the leadership you exhibit, (5) the possibilities on which you focus and try to achieve, (6) the relationships you nurture and maintain, (7) your spirit, and (8) how you channel your passion to flourish. It is as complex as your behavior patterns, motivations, and aspirations.

BIBI is about WHO you are. The Eight Dynamics are about the journey – how you pursue your purpose, have a meaningful impact, and live a fulfilling life. Combining the two is how you flourish. The journey and how you go about it shape WHO you become. All of us change, learn, grow, and evolve during our lifetimes. The direction in which we move and how we conduct ourselves influence our future, which is why the Eight Dynamics play such an important role.

Your direction will ultimately be defined by what inspires you and how you activate your inspiration, passion, and purpose, and the steps you take to launch and continue your journey. Your vision may evolve, and what you bring to fruition may be different from what you envision at the outset. The realities we encounter may alter the course of our path and our outcomes in unanticipated ways. Success in life usually requires that we adapt as circumstances change and as we develop a deeper understanding of what it takes to pursue our purpose. These circumstances may include our goals themselves, our focus and drive to achieve those goals, important relationships, conditions and constraints, and interdependencies. All of these will affect the nature of our journey. The ongoing challenge is to stay true to WHO you are as you morph into the WHO you want to become.

Two Examples

Who is Steve Weitzenkorn and how is his BIBI woven into his personal journey and purpose?

> *The four parts of BIBI reflect who I am, my self-identity. My BIBI, in turn, defines and propels my journey as I live the Eight Dynamics. I apply and integrate one or more parts of my BIBI into each dynamic. As a result, my BIBI and journey are bound together, like an imperfect and roughly cut, eight-faceted gemstone, each repre-*

senting one of the Eight Dynamics. Each facet has depth and emanates light from within because BIBI is at its center. The interior of the diamond represents the core of my being, personal identity, and what I believe.

Here is how my BIBI and my application of the Eight Dynamics are woven together show up in my life.

Core Values: *The values I consciously, if imperfectly, practice include integrity, intellectual honesty, compassion, collaboration, mutual respect, and continual learning. These are integral to my journey, how I interact with others, and conduct myself.* (Beliefs, when practiced, become Behavior.)

Purpose and Vision: *My purpose is to help others live more purposeful, fulfilling, enriching, and contributory lives ... to inspire a world of heartisans. My vision is a universe of inspired people contributing to the greater good and living more purposeful and fulfilling lives.* (Intentions beget Behavior, which leads to Impact.)

My Breath, My Spirit: *I demonstrate these through my good intentions and generosity, reflected through my words and actions; I attempt to project the intangible goodness I feel in my heart through my approach to people and situations, and to model my vision of the future I'd like to help create.* (Beliefs become Intentions, and I breathe life into them through my Behavior.)

Relationships and Engaging Others: *My relationships reflect my priorities of family, friends, causes, and enterprising endeavors. I focus on how I can add value, collaborate, bring cheer, and offer genuine friendship. I develop and nurture relationships across a broad spectrum and focus on those from whom I can learn, support, and engage to promote a greater good. This book is better because of my relationships and the feedback I received about it. Looking forward to the next phase of my journey, I am focused on engaging thousands of people through FindFulfillFlourish.com, speeches, and workshops.* (Behavior leads, ultimately, to Impact.)

Living Possibilities: *I believe that what is possible for me is far greater than I sometimes realize, especially when it involves mobilizing people to perform good works, whether through volunteering, careers, the arts, leadership, politics, sports, philanthropy, or other endeavors. I believe much more is possible in almost every arena, including my areas of expertise, such as organizational consulting experiential learning. My creativity and conceptual skills help define what I can accomplish and how far I can push the bounds of what is possible for me.* (Beliefs become Behavior, which leads to Impact.)

Self-Leadership: *My self-leadership is demonstrated through my initiative to pursue worthy projects. This book and the tools found on the FFF website are recent examples. They help drive my journey and represent new arenas of achievement. I also demonstrate my leadership through community service on boards and committees, in pursuit of a greater good and engaging more people to have a positive impact and live more fulfilling lives.* (Behavior results in Impact.)

Choices: *I am in my third career by choice. The choices I have made throughout my life – from high school to college to graduate school, as well as jobs, family, and the decision to become a self-employed professional – have shaped my journey. Some were easy, some were challenging, and all, collectively, contributed to defining who I am today and the difference I want to make. In my work, I succeed when those I help succeed. I have chosen to apply my knowledge and beliefs to help others infuse their lives with greater meaning and make a positive difference in the areas that resonate with them.* (Intention begets Behavior.)

Passion to Action to Fruition: *I am a doer. Taking action on ideas comes naturally to me, even though there is always a risk involved. Taking the plunge has proven to be very fulfilling, and this book, the accompanying website, and our overall enterprise are the fruition of this initiative. I hope many people benefit from it; if so, that will be the sweetest fruit of my labors.* (Beliefs + Intentions + Behavior = Impact.)

Through my personal interpretation of the Eight Dynamics and explanations of how BIBI works in my life, I still have not necessarily described WHO I really am. I am only an approximation of the BIBI I strive to be and the facets of my journey. The Dynamics do, however, convey WHO I want to be, and how I want to define myself and pursue my journey. Yet I constantly fall short. However, I continually and consciously work to realize my vision of myself and the future I want to create. Each day, more and brighter light reflects off each facet emanating from the center of my BIBI, the stone as a whole, and the WHO I am that evolves as a result.

If I whittle down the answer to the "Who am I?" question into a thirty-second elevator speech, it sounds like this: "I am a values-focused leader who believes in the power of living a purposeful and enriching life, building relationships, pursuing a meaningful vision, and personal innovation. My goal is to help others realize the possibilities of their lives and make a meaningful impact in the world around them. WHO I am is reflected in how I exemplify my beliefs, intentions, and values through my behavior and impact. All of this is integrated into my leadership of the Find Fulfill Flourish project."

Who is Robin Damsky, and how is her BIBI woven into her personal journey and purpose?

To understand WHO I am requires a look at my LifePath. When I was in my early thirties, I began to live a life filled with spirit. When I chose to attend rabbinical school, I embarked on a journey that, over time and from the inside out, has changed my orientation in the world. I went from one that was guided by external teachings to one of life-leadership guided by spiritual values. This change came out of cultivating a relationship with the force I learned to call God — through prayer, study, discussion, and extensive trial and error. I am an infant in this process. Like Steve, I also believe that my manifestation of the Eight Dynamics and BIBI are a work in progress. I find my heart and mind in constant dialogue with what I understand to be God, helping every facet of my being to grow and flourish.

Core Values: *My core values are compassion, trust, integrity, and honesty, working together to make me the best person I can be. I believe in listening to God's voice and in the wise discoveries of so many throughout the ages who have helped make this world a better place.* (Beliefs guide Behaviors, which create Impact.)

Purpose and Vision: *My life and work seem to encompass many purposes, but all contribute to repairing our world. This often comes in the form of guiding individuals to greater self-love and compassion, or helping them make healthy decisions for their lives. My work on the* Find Fulfill Flourish *project is directly related to this vision. At other times, it is directed toward a project or goal that affects a specific community or the world community, like my commitment to protect our earth. My vision is that we can all work together to create communities filled with love and care. My purpose is to partner my imagination and ingenuity with others' to enhance both the communities we touch every day and the more distant ones with which we feel a connection.* (Intentions are fulfilled through our Behavior to create Impact.)

My Breath, My Spirit: *When I breathe in, I feel the neshamah – the soul of the world –breathing into me. I feel the joy of those with lifted spirits and the pain of those in need. You may have heard the famous saying that if one person is suffering in the world, all of us are suffering. My spirit, therefore – my breath of life – helps lift people out of suffering and into joy.* (The Behavior of breath enhances being, which in turn enhances our Impact.)

Relationships and Engaging Others: *Relationships are at the core of everything. When I was thirty, I met a woman who told me that children usually know where their life is heading when they are seven years old. She asked me about my own similar awareness. I'd never seen myself as a flight attendant or model – common aspirations for women when I was a child – but I told her I remember thinking that people should love each other and I wanted to help make that happen. I strive toward this goal for myself and for all those whose lives I touch, as well as the rings that radiate out from* *those relationships. I see in my mind how our world will look when we master this simple – and simultaneously complex – behavior. My engagement with others ranges from guiding them to a self-reflective path of personal growth to working with those already on this path of improving our world. My work on this book is yet one more opportunity to engage others in building loving relationships that will effect a healthier world.* (Beliefs, Behaviors and Intentions are complexly intertwined. Relationships are our testing ground to see how well we are doing at manifesting our Beliefs and ideals.)

Living Possibilities: *I believe my vision of a healthy, whole, loving world is possible, even though some might say it is nothing more than a pipe dream. I have believed in and seen healing and connection where others said it simply couldn't happen. When it comes to my purpose, I never consider the word* can't. *Amazing things are possible if we give ourselves to them fully. This book and the associated tools continue to evolve as Steve and I constantly remain open to new possibilities.* (Belief and Intention together create Impact.)

Self-Leadership: *To have an impact on the world, we first need to be able to guide and heal ourselves. The numerous coaches and teachers in my life were all dedicated to teaching me to be a human becoming, as opposed to simply a human being. From these teachers, I learned to self-reflect and then self-correct. When I gained enough power to guide myself internally, the next step was to use the same tools to guide my actions outward in the world. Jewish teachings enhance this path and help me lead myself in my purpose with insight, care, and compassion.* (Beliefs lead to Behaviors that lead to Impact.)

Choices: *This is both the most exciting and the most challenging of the Dynamics, in my estimation, since endless possibilities exist regarding relationships and work venues. I am choosing how I devote my time, as well as the way I interact in every moment. I consciously choose compassion, understanding, love, and light, even in challenging situations. The result is stronger relationships and community, some of which have well exceeded my expectations. Sometimes I fall* *short of my vision and need to make repairs. Nevertheless, my investments have brought me closer to my vision. It's all about choice.* (Choosing is a Behavior that reflects Intentions and creates an Impact.)

Passion to Action to Fruition: *Passion opens the door to magic in our lives. It is the small glow of fire from my belly that I can hold in my hands. I had to express my passion in many arenas before I was able to reconnect with and live out my simple childhood vision. I find nothing as satisfying as directing my passion toward improving the earth or people's lives, and then seeing the results unfold. My studies gave me tools to use my passion in my work, helping me support individuals and communities to grow and flourish.* (Passionate Behavior, coupled with Intention, leads to Impact.)

Each of us is greater than the sum of our parts. Whether we live the Eight Dynamics more consciously or less consciously, they are all constantly in play. Simply by doing this exercise of attempting to answer the question, "Who am I?" I further crystallized my connection to each dynamic. They work together and strengthen my pursuit of my purpose and my journey. They reflect the complexity of who I am. We are human, which means we are divinely flawed. My goal is not perfection in all these areas, but rather to apply each dynamic as I work toward my vision of helping others build flourishing lives, and to acknowledge growth in myself and others as we walk our paths.

Next Steps in Defining WHO You Are and WHO You Want to Become

Like Alice, many of us struggle with the "Who am I?" question. Begin by asking yourself, "What's my BIBI?" Make that your first step in answering the WHO question for yourself. Then immerse yourself in a purposeful journey toward realizing your vision of the difference you wish to make and WHO you want to become. Use the Eight Dynamics as your personal LifePath GPS system and your BIBI to ground yourself. Remember, your mission is to be true to yourself and your continuing journey. There is always a new LifePath to pursue.

Take advantage of the tools and resources in this book and on the FindFulfillFlourish. com website to find your purpose, fulfill your vision, and live a life that flourishes.

Use the LifePath GPS Exercises as a Trip Plan

The LifePath GPS exercises throughout this book and the additional ones on our website are designed to help you navigate your LifePath and put it in motion or accelerate it.

LifePath GPS is about becoming the you you've always dreamed of becoming, fulfilling your purpose, and enhancing the lives of others. Now your task is to make it happen.

Review of Key Points

- The meaning of our lives evolves from the meaning we pour into it.
- It does not matter where you start, only that you start.
- To find, fulfill, and flourish is a life-long journey.
- Inspiration is activated through the combination of spiritual breathing and purposeful action.
- Your purpose and vision can be as big or as intimate as you'd like – it's about what is right for you.
- A purpose takes on value and meaning through action; the two must work together.
- Living your values is key to achieving your vision. By modeling your values, you emulate the world you envision and bring it a step closer to reality.
- Spirituality is about breathing ... breathing life.
- Healthy, vibrant relationships are integral to living a meaningful and fulfilling life. We open our own lives through relationships with others.
- Engaging others in our purpose gives our work greater momentum and power, and lays the foundation for an ongoing legacy.
- Living possibilities generates positive energy and encourages us to focus on our future achievements and fulfilling our potential.
- Life leadership involves generating and sustaining momentum to pursue a vision and purpose, achieve goals, create

opportunities, and develop and pursue new arenas of
achievement through consistent demonstration of personal
values, proactive
responsibility, and engaging and inspiring others.

- Our choices define who we are and what we become – including
big, life-changing choices, as well as the daily moment-to-
moment choices.
- The "Passion to Action to Fruition" process is key to successfully
traveling the journey to a purpose-guided and fulfilling life.
- Defining WHO you are is a necessary step in becoming and
remaining true to yourself, and flourishing.

The individuals highlighted throughout this book demonstrate unique ways of making this journey, finding their way to becoming heartisans, and establishing their LifePaths. Each of us has our own individual path. While we have matched each story to a key dynamic the individual exhibited on their LifePath, they – like you – each embody all of the concepts, either implicitly or explicitly. They have all activated and pursued a purpose that is deeply meaningful to them. All have established relationships that are instrumental to their success.

Each created – and is continuing to create – a new future for themselves and others, and believes in possibilities. Each incorporates their own understanding of spirituality into their work. Their initiative was the spark that transformed their inspiration into reality. All have confronted obstacles and continue to overcome them regularly. Their choices have forged their identity and created the credibil-ity and momentum for success. All of them discovered, in their own ways, their personal motivations and either consciously or unconsciously integrated those elements into their work and process. Today, they are having an impact, help-ing to create a better world, and are on a LifePath that is deeply meaningful and fulfilling to them.

We began Chapter 2, "The Journey to Find Meaning and Become a 'Hearti-san,'" with a passage from Lewis Carroll's *Alice's Adventures in Wonderland*. As you launch your journey, we leave you this last Carroll passage to reflect on:

"Would you tell me, please, which way I ought to go from here?"

*"That depends a good deal on where you want to get to," said the
Cat.*

"I don't much care where," said Alice.

"Then it doesn't matter which way you go," said the Cat.

"– so long as I get somewhere," Alice added as an explanation.

"Oh, you're sure to do that," said the Cat, "if you only walk long enough."

Unlike directionless Alice, your purpose, vision, and BIBI will serve as the compass for your LifePath, guiding you so that you know where you are going and WHO you are. Your actions will propel you along that road.

Your world and life will become what you make of them, regardless of where you began or where you are now. Your life has meaning when you fill it with meaningful acts. Each of us was born with this capacity – now it's up to you to fulfill your purpose so that you can have a deeply rewarding life.

Travel safely, wisely, passionately, and lovingly – and enjoy the journey!

Think of the world you've always dreamed of.
Once we approach adulthood, we may abandon the dream,
thinking it no longer possible.

What kind of world could we create
if each one of us worked a little bit each day
toward making the world more like the one of our dreams?

If creating the world of our dreams became
an integral part our lives and our legacy to others,
imagine the lives we would touch
and how our own lives would become more meaningful.

*— **Robin Damsky and Steve Weitzenkorn***

APPLYING THE CONCEPTS TO YOUR LIFE

How are each of the Eight Dynamics already working in your life to help you achieve your vision?

Values _____

Purpose/Vision _____

Breath/Spirit _____

Relationships _____

Possibilities _____

Life-Leadership _____

Choices _____

Passion/Action/Fruition _____

What is my BIBI?

My beliefs are ...

My intentions are ...

My behaviors are ...

My impact is ...

Reading Group
Discussion Guide

The questions in this discussion guide are intended to help groups and individuals explore the book's concepts in greater depth and potential applications to their own lives and to those around them. We have selected one or two primary concepts from each chapter; however, you may also wish to discuss the navigational points and questions at the conclusion of each chapter. Our objective is to make *Find Fulfill Flourish* as helpful and valuable as possible.

Chapter 1. The Personal Journey to *Find Fulfill Flourish*

The authors state that "at some point in our lives, we come to the realization that: (a) We are living a life of meaning and purpose, or (b) We are merely being swept along by the tides around us." What are the benefits of living a life of meaning and purpose?

Chapter 2. The Journey to Find Meaning and Become a "Heartisan"

The concepts embedded in this chapter are introduced with a passage from Alice's Adventures in Wonderland, in which Alice is asking, "Who in the world am I?" Later in the chapter the concept of a "heartisan" is introduced. The authors describe heartisans as having a sincere commitment to a worthy cause, which may involve improving the lives of others, their community, or the general well-being. How are the two connected?

Chapter 3. Where to Begin

The book makes the point that it does not matter where you begin your journey of pursuing a purpose. It can begin with action, an idea, a passion, or inspiration from anywhere. The authors also say that the heart is the connector between purpose and action, because purpose without action has no value. How do you interpret this sentence? What have you experienced in your life and how has your heart shown through as a result of purposeful action?

Chapter 4. Values: You Are What You Value

The story of Zuhdi Jasser is intended to illustrate how values and the courage of convictions can propel a powerful personal journey. What role do you believe values should play in a person's life? How are values and the courage of convictions intertwined? What should we do when we discover our actions do not reflect our values?

Chapter 5. Inspired Direction: Purpose, Vision, and Action

The authors explain that a personal purpose can be developed by (1) identifying what one cares about and wishes to address; (2) determining what one values; and (3) determining how one can create meaning and fulfillment for onself. Why are all three important? What might happen if one or more were missing? Can you see the synergy or interplay of these three elements anywhere in your life? If so, how?

Chapter 6. Spirituality: If You Breathe, You're Spiritual

There are many routes to spirituality, including a broad number of religious and non-religious paths. Organized religion offers philosophical and spiritual guidance for many and can play a vital role. Each of us can express our spirituality in our own unique way. The Dalai Lama has said, "There is no need for temples; no need for complicated philosophy. Our own brain, our own heart is our temple; the philosophy is kindness." What does this quote mean to you and do you agree? Why or why not?

Whether you have a religious path or are more secular, how do you apply your spirituality?

Chapter 7. Relationships: Why You Need Others and Others Need You

Dr. Joshua Haberman said, "Many of us are locked inside ourselves. We wonder, what is our purpose? What is our reason for existence? We go through life looking for the key to unlock life. And we never find it – because nobody has the key to his own life. We should be looking for it beyond ourselves, because the meaning of our life is disclosed to us only in our relationship to others." How does this insight connect to discovering one's purpose and living a fulfilling life?

The authors say that the larger one's vision, the greater the need to engage others. Why is this important? What do you believe are the biggest barriers to engaging others and how might they be overcome?

Chapter 8. Living Possibilities: Making the Impossible Possible

George Barnard Shaw is quoted as saying. "The reasonable man adapts himself to the conditions that surround him ... The unreasonable man adapts surrounding conditions to himself ... All progress depends on the unreasonable man." This is a very strong statement. What is the point you feel he is trying to make? What does it have to do with living possibilities and "making the impossible possible?" Have you ever found yourself living out this concept? If so, what were the advantages and obstacles you faced?

Chapter 9. Life Leadership: The First Person You Must Lead Is Yourself

Life leadership refers to the ability to take initiative to guide your life and activities toward achieving your vision in the process of finding personal fulfillment and meaning. It involves transforming your vision and purpose into reality. Why do you think it's important to lead yourself first? How can life leadership be demonstrated in a local community or organization?

Chapter 10. Choices: Change Your Choices, Change Your Life

The authors say that our choices largely define who we are and demonstrate our character. They also discuss the impact of moment-to-moment choices and choices that alter the direction of our lives. How do you see these two types of choices working together or being intertwined? Can you give examples from your own experience?

Chapter 11. Passion to Action to Fruition

This chapter discussed how external affirmation, intrinsic motivation, and intrinsic satisfaction are elements in propelling one's journey and reaching a level of personal fulfillment. How have you seen these three principles work in your life? How can they be applied to help others along their path?

How is "instantism" an obstacle for moving from passion to action to fruition? How can it get in the way of developing fulfilling life? How can it be overcome?

Chapter 12. Forward Navigation: Who Am I Becoming?

What is the value of defining and living one's BIBI (beliefs, intentions, behavior, and impact) to living a fulfilling and confident life?

How are BIBI and the Eight Dynamics woven together in your life?

Let us know about any additional insights or ideas that arise from your discussions. Simply visit the Contact Page at FindFulfillFlourish.com and send us an email.

Index

Author Bios

Steve Weitzenkorn, Ph.D., has more than 25 years' experience as a business and nonprofit advisor, concentrating on the people side of organizational development, leadership, strategy formation, and change. He is a learning innovator and experienced facilitator who has designed programs to improve leadership, trust, strategy implementation and communication, breakthrough interactions, service, and sales effectiveness. Steve donates about 25 percent of his time to helping nonprofits grow and innovate. His programs and simulations have been recognized internationally, including winning the Henkel Award for Global HR Excellence and the Byham Award for Innova-  tion and Excellence in Training Technology. His doctorate is in human learning, with an emphasis on organizational behavior. He has a master's degree in counseling psychology. Steve and his wife live in Arizona where their son is completing his college education.

Robin Damsky is the rabbi of West Suburban Temple Har Zion in River Forest, Illinois. Her work is devoted to guiding individuals and communities to live ethical lives utilizing faith-based teachings. She works both within and across faith and ethnic lines to build relationships that break down barriers between individuals, organizations, and peoples. Robin's years as a professional dancer and medical massage therapist have inspired her vision of a joyful, purposeful and healthful life. Robin earned her rabbinic ordination from the Ziegler School of Rabbinic Studies at American Jewish University, and has two master's degrees: one in Jewish education and one  in rabbinical studies. Robin's articles have been published in various periodicals across the country. A single mother, she understands the challenges of balancing a busy life with pursuing a passion. Her daughter, Sarah, is a freshman at New York University.

Use Coupon Code GBC3MN24
to claim your free membership
to the FindFulfillFlourish.com
website and access all
the activities and tools
mentioned throughout the book.

This book is part of a larger endeavor to guide people to more fulfilling and meaningful lives. The *Find Fulfill Flourish* Project includes special features, tools, and fundraising programs to help individuals and organizations to flourish.

Helping People Flourish

Purchasing this book will give you access to engaging tools, exercises, and supplemental content on our website, FindFulfillFlourish.com. These include:

- **LifePath GPS Survey:** Identify where you are on your journey toward the life you want to experience.
- **Guiding Values Exercise:** Use this electronic exercise to help you identify your most important values.
- **Heartisan Pathfinder Exercise:** Determine your personally meaningful purpose and learn ways to pursue it.
- **Blog:** Read thought-provoking and inspirational posts.
- **Opportunities to share best practices** and ideas.
- **Recognition of "heartisans":** Nominate people you admire who genuinely make a difference.

Helping Organizations Flourish

Because we believe in giving back and paying forward, we offer several ways to help organizations grow and rise to greater heights.

- **Partnership Program.** Generate donations through sales from people you refer to FindFulfillFlourish.com.
- **Fundraising Project.** Purchase books wholesale and resell them at the retail price. The book is an inspirational item for gift stores and fundraising drives.
- **Organizational Membership Program.** Offer your members, employees, students, and supporters memberships to our website at a steep discount, giving them access to exclusive content and exercises.
- **Workshops/Presentations.** Work with us to plan inspirational, thought-provoking programs that can double as fundraisers.
- **Organizational Application Guide.** Leaders and board directors, apply the Eight Dynamics from the book to strengthen your organizations.

More information about all of these *Find Fulfill Flourish* Project features is available on our website. Join our community and take advantage of all we have to offer. We wish you the best on your journey! **FindFulfillFlourish.com**

Made in the USA
Charleston, SC
10 March 2011